GREAT BRITAIN

IRELAND

Grand Tours of the World

GREAT BRITAIN
·
IRELAND

ISAAC & MILLER PUBLISHING LTD.
MONTREAL

ACKNOWLEDGMENTS

Grand Tours of the World
GREAT BRITAIN & IRELAND

Published by
ISAAC & MILLER PUBLISHING LTD.
1 Place Ville Marie
Suite 1918
Montreal, Quebec
H2B 2C3

Original French edition *Beautés du Monde* produced by
LIBRAIRIE LAROUSSE
Editors: Suzanne Agnely, Jean Barraud, J. Bonhomme, N. Chassériau, L. Aubert-Audigier
Designers: A.-M. Moyse, N. Orlando, E. Riffe, H. Serres-Cousiné
Copy editors: L. Petithory, B. Dauphin, P. Artistide
Cartographer: D. Horvath

English edition edited & designed by
ST. REMY PRESS
Editor: Kenneth Winchester
Art director: Pierre Léveillé
Designers: Philippe Arnoldi, Odette Sévigny
Picture researcher: Michelle Turbide
Contributing editors: David Dunbar, Barbara Peck, Madeleine Delpech-Ward
Contributing researchers: Mary Ashley, Jane Ashley McConnell, Katherine Zmetana
Systems manager: Shirley Grynspan

Copyright © Isaac & Miller Publishing Ltd. 1986.
Copyright © Librairie Larousse 1979 for the French edition.

All rights reserved. No part of this book may be reproduced, stored in a retrieval system, or transmitted, in any form or by any means, electronic, photocopying, recording, or otherwise without the prior permission of the Publishers.

Published simultaneously in the United States by Torstar Books Inc.,
and in Canada by Isaac & Miller Publishing Ltd.

Printed in Belgium

ISBN 2-89149-359-1

CONTENTS

Discovering Great Britain & Ireland 7

GREAT BRITAIN 11

Gliding Down the Thames 12

Bright Lights and Big Ben 16

Pilgrims and Conquerors 23

Shakespeare's England 31

Castles and Coal 44

SCOTLAND 51

The Bonnie Lowlands 52

A Highland Fling 56

WALES 64

IRELAND 71

A Georgian Jewel 73

Bastions and Blarney 77

ULSTER 88

Great Britain & Ireland: 90
  A Visitor's Guide

Photography Credits 94

DISCOVERING
GREAT BRITAIN · IRELAND

Great Britain and Ireland echo with the sounds of history: the ring of swords on a lonely battlefield, ethereal voices reverberating through a majestic cathedral, the skirl of bagpipes, the baying of hounds, the rattle of horsedrawn carriages. A crumbling townhouse down this cobblestoned street is the birthplace of a famous writer; an English king lies entombed in that historic church; the ghost that haunts a gloomy castle has roamed its halls for centuries.

Great Britain comprises the large island on which England, Scotland and Wales are situated, as well as a scattering of smaller islands: the Channel Islands, the Isle of Man, the Orkneys, Hebrides and Shetlands. The United Kingdom is made up of Great Britain and Northern Ireland, which shares the island of Ireland with the Republic of Ireland to the south.

Though small in physical size, these verdant isles have wielded enormous influence through the ages. The town of Canterbury is the cradle of English Christianity; the historic document signed in 1215 at Runnymede laid the foundations of modern democracy. Scottish lore and legends have traveled throughout the world in the poems of Robert Burns and tales of the Loch Ness monster, while half of North America pretends to be Irish on St. Patrick's Day.

Proud of their glorious past, the people of Britain and Ireland strive to preserve the old ways. In emerald-green pastures framed by ancient loose-stone walls, shaggy border collies still play nip and tuck with fractious sheep, while old-fashioned country gardens bloom before

thatched-roof cottages, and an evening's entertainment is no farther away than the local pub. Tradition and pageantry enliven London Town: the colorful Changing of the Guard before Buckingham Palace, soapbox orators at Hyde Park's Speakers' Corner, the croak of ravens at the Tower of London, the tolling of Big Ben. And the Scottish, Welsh and Irish have retained many of the centuries-old customs that make their heritages distinct from that of England.

The landscapes of these islands are almost as rich and varied as the history and culture of the people who live here. England's southwestern peninsula is dominated by Dartmoor and Exmoor, two wild, heather-clad expanses of moorland and forest. In the southeast rise the chalky parapets of the White Cliffs of Dover; to the north near London are gently rolling hills called the Downs.

Though parts of the Midlands have been marred by industry, the countryside retains much of its beauty; while in the Lake District soft hills encircle gemlike lakes and charming villages.

Scotland is famous for the lonely peaks and moors of the Highlands, but the grassy pastures and green valleys of the Scottish Lowlands are just as pleasing to the eye. Many consider rugged southwestern Wales to have the most spectacular coastline in Britain, in contrast to Ireland's gentle southern shore. Green pastures and whitewashed cottages are its traditional image, but Ireland also has stark mountains and sparkling lakes.

While most of these landscapes have remained the same for centuries, the populations of Great Britain and Ireland are slowly evolving. The stereotype English gentleman in pin-striped suit and bowler hat now shares the streets of London with white-robed Arabs, turbaned Sikhs and Hong Kong businessmen. Like the Celts, Romans and Norsemen who came before them, these newcomers will surely write fresh pages in the history books of these storied isles.

GREAT BRITAIN

"This sceptered isle . . .
This other Eden, demi-paradise . . .
This precious stone set in a silver sea . . .
This blessed plot, this earth, this realm,
this England."

Shakespeare was writing about England but the spirit of his pen surely embraces Scotland and Wales, the other countries that comprise this island nation. Small in area and population, Britain is astonishingly well endowed in natural beauty, history and culture.

We tend to think of the British as a homogeneous race. But in fact they are a rich mix of different peoples. Over the centuries each wave of invaders left its mark. The Roman's handiwork can still be seen in the arrow-straight roads built to ease the army's advance and in the stones of

Hadrian's Wall. The mysterious ruins of Stonehenge are reminders of the Druid priests of the Celtic era. Fortress-like castles bear witness to the Norman determination to hold fast the power they had won. And the English language—richly woven threads of Latin, French, Germanic and Celtic—is an amalgam of all the tongues that have been spoken here. Freed from fear of invasion since 1066, the British have had the luxury of almost 1,000 years in which to forge a common identity. Small wonder that they think of themselves as a breed apart. For despite Britain's nearness to the Continent, the British savor their insularity. Their proud island mentality reveals itself in the newspaper headline announcing: "Fog in Channel, Continent Isolated."

Throughout the country, however, distinct regional differences do exist. The working-class Cockney of East London can be hard pressed to decipher what a "Geordie" from Newcastle is saying. The Welsh language is still the mother tongue in many parts of Wales, and even today some Scots speak only Gaelic.

But all Britons share a love for the natural beauty of their country, ranging from the sea-lashed headlands of Cornwall to the misty fens of Cambridgeshire; from the winding river valleys of Wales to the windswept Yorkshire dales; from Kent's cherry orchards to the barren Scottish moors and highlands. And all this in a land that has given the world the tradition of democracy, the plays of Shakespeare and the music of the Beatles.

▲ *Eton: Sporting straw boaters bedecked with flowers, students at England's most exclusive public school hold tight to the traditions of their venerable institution.*

Gliding Down the Thames

Many consider the Cotswolds, an enchanting region where tranquil valleys thread past gentle limestone hills thick with ancient oak, to be the most "English" part of England. Here the noble River Thames begins its stately descent to the sea—though the exact location of its birthplace is disputed. Its source is said to be Thames Head, some three miles from the Cotswold village of Cirencester, but in fact this spot is usually dry. Somewhere in the region, however, begins a thin trickle that swells into the historic waterway flowing 146 miles through the heart of England. As recently as 1950 the river was so badly polluted that it was considered dead, but an intense cleanup campaign has met with such success that the Thames is now one of the world's cleanest urban waterways.

The early Romans transformed the Cotswolds into rich farmland. But the region's most enduring treasure lies in the very hills themselves: the limestone rock which once provided the region's main construction material. Throughout the Cotswolds, cottages, churches, gabled barns and weathered stone walls glow with the mellow, honey-brown limestone quarried here.

Even the most modest Cotswold village boasts an imposing church. Of the one in Lechlade, on the upper Thames, Shelley wrote that its "pinnacles point from one shrine like pyramids of fire!" In nearby Fairford, a 15th-century church is adorned with 28 contemporary stained-glass windows illustrating scenes from the Old and New Testaments.

Not far from Lechlade the Thames becomes navigable, lazily winding through lush fields and past picturesque villages. Its willow-shaded banks have inspired generations of writers, and set the stage for such tales as *The Wind in the Willows*, wherein one of Kenneth Grahame's furry characters remarks blissfully, "There is nothing—absolutely nothing—half so much worth doing as simply messing about in boats."

Embraced by the Thames and Cherwell rivers are the "dreaming spires" of Oxford, a precious part of England's cultural heritage. This university city is also a fast-growing manufacturing center, but fortunately its industrial growth has not sullied its historic core. The university buildings, which cover less than one square mile, represent virtually every English architectural style from the 11th century on. The rolling lawns have flourished under centuries of painstaking care, safeguarded by signs specifying who may set foot upon them—usually dons, sometimes students, and never tourists.

Oxford's lifeblood—its young scholars—faithfully uphold the university's countless historic traditions, wearing gowns during exam time or adding their voices to the Christ Church choir. Not all Oxford traditions are serious: scholars swim in the buff at "Parson's Pleasure" in the icy Cherwell River, and at the end of May take to the Thames in raucous races.

Even more competitive boating takes place farther down the Thames at Henley, site of the annual Henley Royal Regatta—the grand prix of race rowing. The Regatta is as much a social event as a sporting one. Onlookers, many in well-preserved antique skiffs, punts and canoes, dress in Edwardian elegance, with white linen and straw boaters.

Later in the summer another annual ritual takes place in Henley. For at least 800 years, the swans that nest along the Thames have been designated as royal birds. Half the swans belong to the Queen; the other half are owned by two London guilds, the Vintners and the Dyers. The annual rite called "Swan Upping" is an attempt to determine "the ownership of all new cygnets encountered on the Thames between London and Henley." Representatives of the three groups set out from London in six skiffs rowed by oarsmen in red, blue and white jerseys.

Below Henley, on the north bank of the ever-widening Thames, stands the historic town of Eton. Here the ancient institution of Eton College, founded in 1440 by 18-year-old Henry VI, has educated some of England's best and brightest men. Today's students, attired in formal tailcoats and striped trousers, can take as their role models such illustrious Eton alumni as the Duke of Wellington (who once remarked, "The battle of Waterloo was won on the playing fields of Eton").

Just across the Thames from Eton rise the towers and battlements of Windsor Castle, the home of English kings and queens for more than 850 years. It was founded on this spot by William the Conqueror in 1066 after his victory at the Battle of Hastings, and added to by succeeding generations of royalty. In fact, the castle's very existence is a physical reminder of the growth of the British nation: crenellated walls and towers built by Norman kings surround the later additions by the Plantagenets, the Tudors, the Stuarts and the Hanovers.

St. George's Chapel, the finest example of perpendicular architecture in England, was completed during the reign of Henry VIII, who also built the great gateway which bears his name. He now shares a tomb in the chapel with his favorite wife, Jane Seymour, and a more unlikely bedfellow, Charles I. The imposing Round Tower, one of the castle's most striking structures, dates from the 12th century, but the huge hollow crown which gives the tower its shape was added by King George IV during his reign in 1820-1830.

▲ *Oxford: Taking a break from the travails of learning, students stroll through one of the city's many patches of green.*

▶ *Most English of countrysides, the Cotswolds near Oxford offer peace and charm as far as the eye can see.*

When Queen Elizabeth II is in residence, the Royal Standard flies from a 72-foot flagpole atop the tower, signifying that the State Apartments are off-limits to tourists. The Queen uses the castle more than any previous sovereign. No doubt she has happy memories here; it was at Windsor that she spent much of her childhood and was wooed by Prince Philip of Greece.

Windsor's priceless array of artworks includes porcelain, tapestries, paintings by Rubens, Holbein and Rembrandt, and drawings by Leonardo da Vinci and Michelangelo. Children of all ages marvel at the magnificent dollhouse given to Queen Mary in 1924. This mansion in miniature has every convenience of the day, including a functioning vacuum cleaner, servants' elevator, and hot and cold running water, as well as a fully operational piano, walnut furniture upholstered in silk damask, and a fleet of cars—all at a scale of one inch to a foot.

Soon after the Thames flows out of sight of Windsor it passes Runnymede, and the famous meadow where, in 1215, rebellious feudal barons forced King John to sign the Magna Carta ("Great Charter"), prosing liberty for his subjects. Farther downriver lies Hampton Court palace, a mellow, red-brick castle built as an opulent private residence by Cardinal Wolsey in 1514, then taken over by Henry VIII. The palace owes its present appearance to the renowned architect Sir Christopher Wren, who altered its design to more closely resemble the palace of Versailles. From here the Thames flows but a short distance to reach the capital city, the heart of England.

◄ *Eton: Bastion of tradition, Eton College requires all students to dress in formal attire. Here, future gentlemen leave a class wearing tailcoats and starched white collars.*

▲ Windsor Castle: The Long Walk, lined with chestnut and plane trees, leads to this ancient home of English kings and queens. From left: the Round Tower, built by Henry II and added to later by George IV; the Edward III tower; the King George IV Gateway, flanked by the Lancaster and York towers; and the massive, square Victoria Tower.

Bright Lights and Big Ben

From green, peaceful countryside the Thames meanders into London, a sprawling, cosmopolitan city that has witnessed 2,000 years of pageantry and tradition. "When a man is tired of London, he is tired of life, for there is in London all that life can afford," wrote Samuel Johnson 200 years ago. The saying is no less true today; the modern visitor to this city finds a treasure trove of history, of stately squares and monuments, of architectural wonders, of leafy parks and tempting shops, of theaters and museums and fascinating people.

When Londoners speak of "The City," they mean only a portion of London—the square mile that extends back to Roman and medieval times. This area was once a walled city, and still retains certain self-governing rights. The City shows its age in the remains of its Norman walls; its narrow, winding streets; and the rich history embedded in the stones of the venerable Tower of London. Every time a new foundation is dug here, workmen unearth artifacts that date as far back as 2,000 years to Roman Londinium.

In fact, the London of today is not one city, but a patchwork of towns that over the centuries were swallowed up one by one as the city grew. Many of these villages, such as Chelsea, retained their original character, thus creating a hybrid city of distinct neighborhoods. This conglomeration, though confusing to tourists, gives London its special charm.

Many tours of London begin at venerable Trafalgar Square, a pigeon-filled, fountain-splashed precinct named for the naval battle in which Lord Nelson won a decisive victory against Napoleon in 1805, yet lost his own life. Nelson is commemorated here by an immense statue atop a towering pedestal that is guarded at its base by four huge bronze lions—favorite perches for photographed visitors.

Not far from Trafalgar Square, stands Buckingham Palace, official residence of Queen Elizabeth II. When Her Majesty is at home, the Royal Standard waves from the flagpole. Whether she's there or not, the famous soldiers stand guard in their scarlet tunics and weighty bearskin hats called busbies. One of London's most popular pageants takes place with the Changing of the Guard, in summer a daily ceremony of intricate drill movements.

Only a few blocks from Buckingham Palace the twin spires of Westminster Abbey soar heavenward. Ever since William the Conqueror chose the new, incomplete abbey as the site for his crowning in 1066, it has been the scene of the coronation, marriage and burial of British monarchs through the centuries. One of the nation's finest Gothic buildings, it houses the graves of most of the sovereigns from Henry III to George II. Some of England's greatest literary heroes are buried in its Poet's Corner, including Chaucer, Ben Jonson, Browning, and Tennyson. Lord Byron was added only lately due to his scandalous life; Longfellow is the sole American laid to rest here. The Abbey also houses the Coronation Chair, made in 1300 for the crowning of Edward I, and still used to install new monarchs.

▲ London: With its magnificent, 365-foot dome, St. Paul's Cathedral looks more like a palace than a church. Inside its crypt are the massive tombs of Lord Nelson and the Duke of Wellington.

◄ London: Since the coronation of William the Conqueror in 1066, all British sovereigns have been crowned beneath the soaring Gothic arches of Westminster Abbey.

Almost next door, the massive bulk of the Houses of Parliament stretches 940 feet along the west bank of the Thames. Both the House of Commons and the House of Lords meet here in what was once the royal Palace of Westminster. All of London sets its watches by the celebrated Big Ben, perhaps the city's most enduring symbol. In fact, the name refers not to the clock, but to the 13.5-ton bell which chimes within the clock tower. Also in the tower are cells intended to confine MPs for any breach of Parliamentary privilege. The last one so imprisoned was in 1880—which may surprise today's tourists in the Commons Visitors Gallery, who witness the lively debate that sometimes degenerates into raucous heckling.

In 1666 the Great Fire ravaged London, sweeping away three-quarters of the medieval city. In the City, a Gothic cathedral named St. Paul's was destroyed, and the King asked architect Christopher Wren to design a new cathedral to stand in its place. The result was the new St. Paul's—one of the world's great churches and the crowning achievement of Wren's illustrious career. Rather than a tower or spire, a great stone cupola tops the immense cruciform structure. It was the first dome in England, reminiscent of such great Renaissance churches as St. Peter's in Rome.

St. Paul's has been the scene of many notable events in English history, most recently the wedding of Prince Charles and Lady Diana Spencer in 1981. Among the notables buried within the cathedral's hallowed walls is its architect, upon whose tomb is engraved in Latin: "Here lies Sir Christopher Wren. If you would see his monument, look around you."

Few visitors to this city miss a trip to the Tower of London, which is said to be the world's most-visited historic site. Indeed, lore and legend seem to seep from the very stones of this mighty fortress, and the smiling, mustachioed Yeomen Warders, or "Beefeaters," who guard the Tower hold visitors spellbound with gory tales of its macabre past. (Beef has nothing to do with the name of these Tudor-costumed gentlemen; their company was founded in 1485 as the *boufitiers* or guardians of the King's buffet.)

▲ *London: Britain's stately Houses of Parliament are seen to best advantage from across the Thames. The Union Jack flying from Victoria Tower on the left means Parliament is in session.*

William the Conqueror built the great stone White Tower here in 1077, as much to encourage the loyalty of his new subjects in England as to defend them. Later rulers added stone walls, more towers and fortified gates, eventually producing the stronghold we see today. Over the years the Tower has been a prison, a palace, a museum, an armory and a treasure chest. Two of Henry VIII's ill-fated wives, Anne Boleyn and Catherine Howard, were held here before being led to the scaffold. Beefeaters point to the very spot where Anne Boleyn's head was separated from her body, the deed being done by a French sword instead of the usual English ax.

Tradition holds that the Bloody Tower here was the site of the murder of the little princes—according to Shakespeare, killed by their uncle, Richard III, in 1485. Here, too, Sir Walter Raleigh was imprisoned for 13 years. Two rooms are furnished as they might have been when he was here. In the walls of the Beauchamp Tower can still be seen despairing graffiti carved centuries ago by suffering prisoners.

Inside the imposing White Tower a priceless collection of medieval arms and armor is displayed. Four metal suits of armor once worn by Henry VIII—each one larger than the last—bear witness to that self-indulgent monarch's increasing girth over the years. An even more valuable and impressive display can be seen in the Tower's Jewel House. Under heavy guard, the precious gems of England's Crown Jewels flash and gleam.

▲ *London: The British pub is a way of life, and sharing a pint in the local watering hole, along with a hearty pub meal and perhaps a game of darts, is almost the national pastime.*

► *London: Scarlet symbols of tradition, a Grenadier from the regiment guarding Buckingham Palace confers with a Yeoman Warder, or Beefeater, from the Tower of London.*

The Coronation Robes, covered in gold embroidery, pale in comparison to the other items traditionally used by every monarch during the investiture: King Edward's Crown, a five-pound, jewel-encrusted piece originally made for Charles II's coronation in 1660; and the Royal Sceptre, which contains the world's largest diamond—the 530-carat "Star of Africa" from the Cullinan diamond found in 1905.

Even the birds that haunt the fabled Tower are a source of legend. Six ravens here are registered as official Tower residents, and are fed a daily ration of six ounces of meat. Legend has it that they are descended from birds who have lived within the Tower for more than nine centuries—and that if ever they should leave, the Tower will fall.

► *London: Though it looks harmless in sunlight, the Tower of London harbors sinister memories. Through the Traitor's Gate, boats bearing prisoners entered the fortress, carrying their passengers to their doom.*

► *London: The Tower Bridge spans a bustling waterway. Its drawbridge lifts to allow large ships up the Thames. A recent renovation restored the two high walkways between the towers, long closed to the public.*

▲ *London: Her parks are her pride and joy. These citizens are enjoying a game of lawn bowling on one of the many oases of green that are called "the lungs of London."*

ENTRY TO THE TRAITORS' GATE

History of a less violent kind can be seen in the venerable British Museum, one of the world's largest. Here are the legendary Elgin Marbles, which once graced the Parthenon in Athens; as well as the Rosetta Stone, whose inscriptions provided the long-sought key to interpreting hieroglyphics. The museum's manuscript room displays the original Magna Carta, Leonardo da Vinci's sketchbook, and the First Folio edition of Shakespeare's plays (1623).

The immense National Gallery houses Britain's national collection of paintings, including representative works by every European master for the past 600 years. British art, both traditional and contemporary, is the specialty of the Tate Gallery, which displays Gainsborough landscapes in one section, and David Hockney's portraits in another.

While a glimpse of traffic-choked Piccadilly Circus might lead any visitor to think that a patch of green is a rare sight in London, the city is in fact famous for its parks. Royal decrees preserved acres of land for deer hunting—land which has since become public parks. Hyde Park is the largest, adjoining Kensington Gardens to offer a square mile of velvety lawns, shade trees and flowerbeds. Anglers fish in the Serpentine, a lake which winds through the park, while rowers glide by.

England's finest flowers thrive at the Royal Botanic Gardens in Kew, just outside London. Gigantic conservatories harbor shrubs, flowers and trees from all over the world; huge flowerbeds display masses of roses and rhododendrons.

Englishmen love gardens, and those who can't be near a garden make their own—even if it's only a window box. Every spring London gardeners gather at the Chelsea Flower Show, a four-day horticultural event that even the Queen tries not to miss. Generations of artists and writers have made this area their home, and visitors with a keen eye for the blue plaques erected by the Historical Society to designate historic and literary landmarks, will spot many on the streets of Chelsea. Past residents have included Oscar Wilde, Henry James, and T.S. Eliot.

Chelsea's trendy boutiques, a main attraction for many visitors, range all the way from chic to punk. But for one-stop shopping, none rivals Harrods, London's grand old lady of department stores. Situated in fashionable Knightsbridge, an exclusive neighborhood of luxury shops and high-priced hotels, this giant emporium is said to be the world's largest department store. Harrods' food section offers more than 500 varieties of cheese alone; not far away is a selection of sinful confections presented in displays that are elegant works of art.

London's nightlife offers a wealth of pleasures, too. Soho, though somewhat drab by day, comes alive at sundown, as audiences flock to movies and live theater, garish neon lights up the night, and jazz clubs and discotheques open their doors. Until 11 p.m., London's pubs—and there are some 7,000 of them—are the best places to mingle with the locals. Even a tiny hole-in-the-wall may have existed in the same spot for a hundred years, its decor of velvet curtains and etched glass barely changed over the decades, and its mahogany bar polished to a fine patina by generations of elbows hoisting the traditional pint of bitter.

◄ *London: The densely packed streets of the Soho district are famous for their fashionable restaurants, offbeat shops and seedy nightlife.*

▲ *London: Two bobbies direct tourist traffic on King's Road in Chelsea. Their nickname comes from Sir Robert Peel, founder of the Metropolitan Police Force.*

► *London: Half a dozen streets radiate from Piccadilly Circus. The figure atop the bronze fountain is known to Londoners as Eros, Greek god of love—but is actually the Angel of Charity.*

Pilgrims and Conquerors

In the heart of the town of Canterbury, southeast of London, lies Canterbury Cathedral, the cradle of English Christianity. The long grey cathedral is the Mother Church of Anglicans throughout the world. For more than 300 years it was also a place of pilgrimage to the shrine of England's martyr-saint, Thomas à Becket, who was murdered here in 1170, just one century after the cathedral's founding. Becket, the 40th Archbishop of Canterbury, was slain by four henchmen of Henry II after years of struggles with the king over who was the final authority on church matters. Soon after his death he was canonized, and pilgrims from all over the world flocked here to honor him. Chaucer immortalized these pilgrimages in the 14th century when he wrote *Canterbury Tales,* the bawdy classic in which each pilgrim relates his story as the group journeys toward the shrine.

In 1538 Henry VIII put a stop to it all. He issued a writ denouncing Becket for treason and rebellion, and ordered all traces of the shrine removed. But 12 stained-glass windows depicting miracles Becket is said to have performed managed to escape destruction, and have also survived two world wars, during which time they were removed for safety.

Sections of the splendid, Gothic-style cathedral were damaged during World War II, and part of the town of Canterbury also suffered from German bombardments in 1942. Nevertheless, much of its medieval character has been retained. After the cathedral, Canterbury's most imposing historic building is the Westgate, sole survivor of seven former gates to this once walled city. For many years the Westgate served as a prison; today it houses a museum that recalls its grisly past in displays of arms and armor, shackles and instruments of torture.

Canterbury is the capital of Kent, a rich, fertile county of orchards and market gardens. Kentish horizons are punctuated by oast-houses: tall, conical buildings where the hops used in brewing beer are dried. In May the county is pastel pink and white with acres of apple and cherry blossoms. In an England full of gardens, Kent is called "the garden of England."

The scenery changes in north Kent, where lively seaside resorts capitalize on their broad sandy beaches and—for England—long hours of sunshine. This area is popular with holidaying Londoners, and for years the towns of Margate and Ramsgate have indulged in friendly rivalry over the local tourist trade. Charles Dickens spent many summers in the resort town of Broadstairs; it was here that he wrote *David Copperfield.*

The rolling meadows called the North Downs end at the sea with the famous White Cliffs of Dover. At one end of the shortest route between England and the Continent, Dover is the rallying point for millions of travelers aboard the ferries, hovercraft and hydroplanes that swarm across the narrow Strait of Dover. The view from Dover Castle, a Norman stronghold high atop the chalky cliffs, is magnificent on a clear day.

A vogue for sea bathing which sprang up in the 18th century resulted in the rapid growth of a number of resort towns along the southeast coast in Sussex County, where the air is bracing and the ocean water mild. Hastings was once a fishing port, and the tall wooden huts once used for drying nets still stand by the beach. The nearby town of Battle was built on the site of the Battle of Hastings.

Brighton, England's most famous resort, also began as a fishing town. The Prince of Wales, later George IV, was charmed by Brighton when he first visited

▲ *Canterbury: The central tower of the majestic Canterbury Cathedral, spiritual center of the Anglican Church, is called the Bell Harry Tower after the great bell it houses.*

it in 1783. In 1787 he had a mansion built there, then later had it remodelled into a fantastic Oriental palace—the Royal Pavilion. Many of the Prince's contemporaries attacked its extravagant appearance—the outside Indian, the interior oriental. "The dome of St. Paul's," wrote a satirist of the day, "must have come to Brighton and pupped." But because of the Prince's interest in the town, Brighton became one of the nation's great holiday playgrounds, and remains so to this day.

The center of the county of Hampshire is Winchester, for centuries the capital of England under Saxon and Norman kings. Despite its waning importance, the town remains one of England's historic treasures, with its great Norman cathedral and numerous well-preserved medieval buildings. The Great Hall of Winchester Castle is thought to be the finest in England, after Westminster Hall. In it hangs a massive representation of the Round Table of King Arthur's time, with space for the king and his 24 knights, which was probably crafted in Tudor times.

When William the Conqueror arrived in England, he was so well pleased by its great woodlands that he set aside 90,000 acres in Hampshire as a royal hunting preserve. Besides ancient stands of oak and beech trees, the New Forest covers moor, marsh and heath, where wild animals and some 2,000 New Forest ponies roam. At one time savage laws ensured the forest's protection. A man could be blinded for so much as disturbing a deer. Today, two-thirds of the park is open to the public, and visitors must follow less stringent regulations, giving animals priority on roads.

The Isle of Wight is, like Brighton, essentially a tourist resort, but its atmosphere is distinctly Victorian. It was here on this island that Queen Victoria and Prince Albert built Osborne House. The Queen was to die there in 1901, and visitors will find her cosy sitting room much as she left it. That house, and other Victorian "cottages" built at the time, give the island a lasting appeal for lovers of Victorian architecture.

Tennyson once lived on the Isle of Wight, but moved away because he felt harassed by tourists. No doubt he would feel even more harassed here today, as thousands of visitors come to relax in this sunny England in miniature with its charming bays, thatched villages, roses and honeysuckle.

The chalklands of Salisbury Plain dominate the south of England, and one of the most beautiful cathedral cities in England, Salisbury, lies at the edge of the plain. Unlike Canterbury and other cathedrals that were built piecemeal throughout the Middle Ages, Salisbury Cathedral was conceived and executed in a single style. Begun in 1220 and completed except for its tower and spire by 1258, it has "as many windows as days in the year, as many pillars as hours, and as many gates as moons." The 404-foot spire, the tallest in England, has been immortalized by the artist John Constable.

An equally impressive—yet far more primitive and mysterious—monument to man's handiwork lies to the north at Stonehenge. How were these giant stone monoliths, some more than 20 feet high, placed in two concentric circles, after having been dragged over miles of countryside? And why? To judge by the way various stones are aligned with the midsummer sunrise, Stonehenge may have

been built as a place of worship. Today, Druids in hooded white robes meet here to celebrate their ancient rites before dawn on Midsummer Day.

England's rugged southwestern coast has been shaped by the sea, and nowhere is this more evident than in the cliff-lined north coast of Devon. Here promontories of grey rock drop steeply down to the sea, interspersed with long stretches of sand. This spectacular scenery is best seen at Hartland Point, at the entrance to the Bris-

◄ *Brighton: The onion-shaped dome and Indian-style minarets of the Royal Pavilion reflect the exotic taste of the Prince of Wales who was to become George IV.*

tol Channel, where many ships have been dashed to pieces on the shoals that litter the coast. The nearby town of Clovelly has been called "a village like a waterfall." Its cobblestoned streets are so steep and narrow that cars are banned, and donkeys make daily deliveries to the shops.

Brooding over much of Devon are the great granite uplands of Dartmoor Forest. The largest stretch of wilderness in southern England, this windswept expanse of heather-clad moors, dense woods and

marshy bogs is home to the hardy Dartmoor ponies, related to Stone Age horses who have lived here for millions of years. Dartmoor's stark landscape attracts nature-lovers to its hundreds of miles of public footpaths and hiking trails, while fishermen come to test its streams teeming with trout and salmon. Prehistoric sites are strewn about the hillsides. The region's eerie charm appealed to Conan Doyle, who set *The Hound of the Baskervilles* on Dartmoor's lonely heath.

Another side of Devon is revealed along the county's southern coast. Here, on what is called the "English Riviera," sunbathers bask on golden beaches beneath waving palm trees, and swim in warm waters while tall-masted yachts idle at the wharves of luxury hotels. Thousands of British, Scottish and Welsh holidayers join other tourists each summer in such elegant seaside towns as Torquay, Paignton and Brixham, now amalgamated to form an area called Torbay.

▲ *Dover: Blue skies over the White Cliffs of Dover are often cross-Channel visitors' first or last glimpse of England. The cliffs have been the country's first line of defense since Roman times.*

Exeter, the principal historic city in Devon, was once a frontier town in the Roman occupation, and ancient foundations, mosaics and pavements can still be found here. Exeter Cathedral, the finest building in Devon, was built from the 11th to 14th centuries in elaborate Norman Gothic style. Its west front is covered with a remarkable collection of stone statues; the interior features a vaulted ceiling carved to resemble the radiating branches of a palm tree. Exeter's Maritime Museum displays more than 100 historic ships.

From the port town of Plymouth, young Englishmen have long set off in search of seafaring adventure. Sir Francis Drake sailed from here in 1577 on his famous global circumnavigation; he was also in Plymouth when he received word of the Spanish Armada's impending invasion in 1588. Legend has it that he lingered to finish his game of bowls before attending to the Spaniards; likely, his devil-may-care attitude was due to the timetable of the tides. Others who launched their ships from Plymouth include the Pilgrims in 1620, Captain Cook in 1772, and Sir Francis Chichester in 1966.

Like that of Devon, the Atlantic coast of Cornwall is battered by the sea. Thundering breakers have carved stark cliffs and jagged rocks in the coastline around Tintagel, a romantic seaside town where the legend of Camelot comes alive. There is no archaeological evidence to support

▲ *Dartmoor: Shaded streams that wind through the green valleys of the park shelter trout and the occasional salmon.*

▲ *Dartmoor: The shaggy ponies that roam this rugged national park are no longer wild; the local farmers who own them hold an annual "pony drift" each fall to round them up.*

▶ *Selworthy: In this town near Lynton and Lynmouth, traditional, white-painted, thatched cottages stand on a wooded hillside at the edge of the wild, high moorland of Exmoor.*

the claim that this is the birthplace of King Arthur, but the great castle whose remains still stand on a rocky cliff is said to be the site where Lancelot and Galahad sat with the other Knights at the Round Table. A cave on the shingle beach below the town is believed to be where Merlin the Magician once lived.

At Land's End, the westernmost point of the English mainland, the cliffs come to an abrupt and craggy halt. On a fine day the Scilly Isles can be seen on the horizon, a cluster of about 100 islands some 25 miles off the coast. The climate is so mild here that spring flowers bloom in November. Only five of the largest islands are inhabited, but boats take visitors to even the loneliest islets, where puffins and seals bask in the sun. Countless ships have run aground here over the centuries, and the seabed is littered with wrecks.

In a dramatic cliff-top setting near Land's End, actors perform Greek, Shakespearian and modern drama at the tiny, open-air Minack Theatre in Porthcurno. The town of Penzance farther down the coast retains the flavor of its seafaring past in the cobblestoned streets of its old quarter. From here fresh flowers and the day's catch of lobster, herring, mackerel and whitefish are shipped to London and points north. Close by is St. Michael's Mount, a huge medieval castle and abbey perched on a rock in Mount's Bay. Historians believe the monastery here was founded in the eighth century, around the

time Celtic monks built a similar structure in France—Mont St. Michel. Though both these unusual sites are surrounded by water at high tide, both can be reached by foot when the tide is out.

Like most Cornish coastal villages, the town of Polperro has a history of smuggling. Today a thriving resort town and fishing center, Polperro recalls its ignominious past with an unusual smuggling museum in the cellar of one of its historic cottages. Artists have long been charmed by the way the town's weathered, whitewashed houses seem to tumble over one another into the small harbor. So popular has the town become that its streets are closed to cars in summer.

A taste of England with a French flavor can be found in the Channel Islands, geographically part of France—they lie just eight miles off the coast of Normandy—but historically possessed by England ever since William the Conqueror, then Duke of Normandy, became King of England in 1066. Jersey and Guernsey are the largest of the six main islands, and both are famous for their distinctive breeds of cattle and their hand-knit sweaters.

On self-governing Jersey, French is the official language, but everyone speaks English. Nevertheless, many of the narrow streets in the main town, St. Helier, have French names, and the restaurants serve fine Gallic fare. In the northeast part of the island, author and naturalist Gerald Durrell has established a unique zoo dedi-

▲ *Stonehenge: Druids bearing mistletoe celebrate the midsummer sunrise at a site where similar ceremonies are believed to have been held 4,000 years before. Sadly, crowds of tourists have now forced authorities to fence off the stones.*

▲ *Hartland Point: Humpbacked ridges of rock reach out to where the coast used to be, as the Devon shoreline gradually recedes under the merciless attack of the Atlantic.*

cated to the breeding of endangered species. Its 20 acres house specimens of such rare animals as lowland gorillas, Tibetan white-eared pheasants and beautifully plumed Egyptian bare-faced ibises.

On Guernsey, still predominantly an agricultural island, vast greenhouses shelter crops of early tomatoes and flowers. The writer Victor Hugo spent 15 years in exile here, but it would seem that it was time well spent. At Hauteville House, which is furnished and maintained just as it was in Hugo's day, the gifted writer penned *Toilers of the Sea* as well as his greatest work, *Les Miserables.*

During World War II the Germans occupied the Channel Islands, and signs of their presence still exist in the grim German Underground Hospital on Guernsey; in Jersey's St. Peter's Bunker, a museum housed in a seven-room German bunker; and in the German blockhouses on the island of Alderney, some of which now serve a more peaceful purpose as vacation cottages.

▲ *Polperro: Fish are still caught from this typical*
▲ *Cornwall seaside village, but most of the boats that leave here in summer carry vacationers in quest of mackerel.*

▲ *St. Michael's Mount: According to legend, this island-at-high-tide is part of the lost kingdom of Lyonesse, where King Arthur's knights once rode.*

Shakespeare's England

The lands to the north and west of London, called the Home Counties, are as scenically varied as anywhere in the country. Though industrial development has marred some of England's natural beauty, manmade landscapes—many to be seen in this area—have managed to, if not restore, at least replace it.

During the 18th century a back-to-nature movement led landscape gardeners to discard the formal, Renaissance style of gardening in favor of something more uniquely English. Rather than neat, geometrical lawns and straight rows of trees, they designed gardens that mirrored nature, using the natural contours of the ground. The movement was partly inspired by the paintings on Chinese porcelain and partly by French landscape artists. Of landscape gardeners, Walpole wrote, "They leaped the fence and saw that all nature was a garden."

A fine example of this great contribution to the art of gardening can be seen at Blenheim Palace, not far from Oxford. Landscape gardener Lancelot Brown, better known by his nickname "Capability," considered the lake he created here to be his masterpiece. The palace and grounds are open to the public. West Wycombe Park, in Buckinghamshire just north of London, is a beautiful Palladian mansion set in grounds landscaped by Humphrey Repton, who aimed at providing panoramic views from each of the house's main windows. Other examples can be seen in Bedfordshire at Luton Hoo, a lavish country house on 1,200 acres laid out by Capability Brown; and at Woburn Abbey, a palatial home that the Duke of Bedford has opened to the public in an effort to keep his family treasures intact.

The city of Birmingham in the West Midlands is a more contemporary example of man's manipulation of the land. With the onset of the Industrial Revolution, Birmingham expanded so rapidly that it soon sprawled over a vast area, factories spewing out black smoke side-by-side with shoddy, overcrowded housing. But in recent years, massive rebuilding has transformed England's second-largest city. A sparkling, white-tiled railway station, an ultra-modern shopping center, and attractive new hotels and office towers create the appearance of a city of the future.

The best of the old remains: the Town Hall, where Birmingham's symphony orchestra performs; historic Aston Hall, a fine Jacobean mansion; and the city's manmade waterways, once the highways of the Industrial Revolution. By 1850, some 5,000 miles of canals formed a network that linked England's four great estuaries—the Mersey, Severn, Trent and Thames—with its new industrial centers in the Midlands and the North. Recent years have witnessed the revival of the canals, and many have been renovated for pleasure boating. Oddly, Birmingham has more canals than Venice.

▲ *Forbidding Durham Castle in northern England has been inhabited for more than 900 years. Today it serves as a university student residence; in summer, a tourist hotel.*

Coventry, in the same mining and industrial area as Birmingham, is another impressive example of man's destructive and creative powers. In a single night in November 1940, German bombs reduced 40 acres of the city center to rubble. Today only the blackened shell of the old cathedral bears evidence of the destruction. Elsewhere, modern new buildings are set amid public parks bright with flowers. A few of Coventry's medieval buildings did survive the war, along with some well-preserved old city gates. A statue here commemorates the famous Lady Godiva, who is said to have ridden naked through the streets of Coventry in an apparently successful effort to persuade her husband to reduce local taxes.

To the north of Coventry, strip mines scar the landscape, and spreading industrial suburbs have swallowed picturesque villages. Green spaces open up to the south, however, punctuated by sites of historic interest. Warwick, a compact county town, barely survived a disastrous fire in 1694. But Georgian houses and a church spire built since that time blend pleasantly with the fine old Tudor buildings that escaped the flames. And beside the Avon River rise the majestic walls and turrets of Warwick Castle rise. Until 1978, this 14th-century castle, converted into a

▲ *Woburn Abbey: The 3,000-acre park surrounding this sumptuous manor house has been turned into a wild animal kingdom, sheltering endangered species of deer from around the world.*

house in the 17th century, was one of the few medieval fortresses to have been continuously inhabited. But the expense of maintenance finally forced the owners to sell to Madame Tussauds Ltd., operators of London's famous waxworks museum. Visitors can stroll through the castle's splendidly decorated State Apartments and shiver at the dungeon's grisly display of torture instruments.

A few miles away is Rugby, today an industrial town of little interest save for its famous public school, founded in 1567. That school gave the world the sport of rugby football, and a plaque on the wall there reads: "This stone commemorates the exploit of William Webb Ellis, who, with a fine disregard for the rules of football as played in his time, first took the ball in his arms and ran with it, thus originating the distinctive feature of the Rugby game A.D. 1823."

It was in Warwickshire that Shakespeare was born, and these tranquil landscapes

▲ *Stratford-upon-Avon: Fine Tudor gables grace Hall's Croft, home of Shakespeare's daughter Susanna and her husband, Dr. John Hall. Its herb garden is the sort a physician would have kept.*

▲ *Warwick: Half-timbered Lord Leycester's Hospital was originally a guildhall in the time of Henry VI, but was converted to a hospital in 1571 —and it sill in use.*

► *Warwick: In a view the novelist Sir Walter Scott considered unsurpassed in England, the battlements of medieval Warwick Castle rise above the River Avon.*

are celebrated in his works. Each year Shakespeare's birthplace in the old market town of Stratford-upon-Avon is visited by an astounding half-million people from all over the world. Part of the half-timbered house on Henley Street where he was born in 1564 is decorated with furnishings typical of Shakespeare's period. The tidy garden in back contains a unique collection of trees, shrubs and flowers that are mentioned in Shakespeare's plays.

Admirers of Shakespeare pay homage to the playwright at other shrines, too. New Place in Stratford, where Shakespeare lived with his wife and children, was demolished in 1759, but its foundations and gardens can still be seen. Hall's Croft, Shakespeare's daughter's home, is open to the public, as are Anne Hathaway's cottage, a short two-mile walk from Stratford, and the home of Mary Arden, Shakespeare's mother, in the nearby village of Wilmcote. Shakespearian plays are at the Royal Shakespeare Theatre from March through November.

Modern transportation and inventions have altered life in Warwickshire since the 16th century, but Shakespeare would recognize the face of the land. Sheep still graze on the hillsides; cattle roam the pastures; the Avon flows quietly past willow-fringed banks. Though little remains of the great Forest of Arden north of Stratford, the setting for *As You Like It,* there are still woodland glades and shady walks that give no hint of nearby Birmingham.

Compton Wyngates, one of the most beautiful houses in England, stands a few miles from Stratford. This stone and weathered-brick mansion was built by the Compton family between 1480 and 1528, largely of materials salvaged from the ruins of Fulbrook Castle near Warwick. The house contains a banqueting hall with a minstrels' gallery, and a priest's hiding hole which was once connected with the moat by an escape route. But the house was seized from its Royalist owners by Cromwell's troops in the Civil War, and later returned to the Comptons only on the condition that the escape route be permanently closed.

To many, the words "North Midlands" conjure up images of grimy smokestacks and rows of identical red-brick houses. While the Industrial Revolution did leave its mark in the mining and manufacturing area pejoratively called the Black Country, the North Midlands have charming villages and broad expanses of rural landscape, as well as the high, rocky crags and moors of the Peak District.

► *Shottery: Set in an English country garden, the thatched "cottage" where Anne Hathaway lived before her marriage to William Shakespeare is actually a 12-room house.*

The ancient market town of Bridgnorth is divided into two parts, a High Town linked to a Low Town on the banks of the Severn by a cliff railway. In 1646 Cromwell's troops blew up the 11th-century Norman castle here and razed most of the town. But the castle keep still stands—though it tilts at an angle three times that of the Leaning Tower of Pisa.

Not far from Bridgnorth, the Severn River flows past the birthplace of the Industrial Revolution—a small town called Iron-Bridge. The graceful 200-foot arch spanning the Severn here was completed in 1781, the first bridge in the world to be made entirely of metal. The builders, ignorant of rivets and bolts, used wooden joints to hold it together. Until this time, charcoal had been the fuel used to smelt iron, and timber was becoming increasingly scarce. A new process that involved smelting iron in blast furnaces fueled with coke—made from local coal—meant that high-quality iron could now be available in quantities previously undreamt of. A museum here tells what happened after this breakthrough: The Iron-Bridge Gorge became a vast industrial complex, producing iron and cast-iron structures of all kinds. Engineers from around the world came to study this innovative process. Though the blast furnaces are silent now, and flowers bloom where smokestacks once belched fumes, the iron bridge still stands, a monument to the pioneers of the Industrial Revolution.

Shrewsbury, a lovely country town standing within a loop of the Severn, boasts an unusual wealth of well-preserved half-timbered buildings. Narrow, winding alleys with crazily tilting houses and such descriptive names as Grope Lane, Butcher Row and Gullet Passage are little changed since Elizabethan days. An illustrious student of the local public school, Charles Darwin, born here in 1809, is commemorated by a statue.

The names Wedgwood, Minton, Spode and Royal Doulton are known worldwide for their fine pottery and porcelain. For the last 300 years, this china has all been made in a corner of North Staffordshire, in five towns with ample supplies of clay, coal and water at their doorstep. The towns were once called "the Potteries," but in 1910 were amalgamated to form the city of Stoke-on-Trent.

In the 1680s the Staffordshire potters made mostly plain, earthenware articles for everyday use. But in 1657 tea was introduced in England, and within a few years tea-drinking was all the rage. The potters

wasted no time in stepping up their production of elegant cups, saucers and teapots so that the rich and fashionable could indulge this new taste. The construction of the Trent and Mersey Canal meant that the fragile wares could be transported with a minimum of breakage, and the flourishing industry began producing china for export to the Continent and North America.

Josiah Wedgwood became a master of the craft, setting up his own business in 1759 and later developing the white relief

work on a blue background for which he is famous. At the Wedgwood Visitor Centre young apprentices demonstrate their craft; a museum displays some of Josiah's handiwork, including one especially intricate masterpiece that took him four years to create.

The Peak District of Derbyshire has some of Britain's most picturesque countryside: bare windswept hills, rugged moors of heather and peat, and lush pastures scored with endless loose-stone walls. Some peaks rise above 2,000 feet, and provide a formidable challenge to even the most experienced rock climbers. Hikers, too, are attracted to this region, for Edale, in the heart of the Peak District National Park, marks the start of the famous Pennine Way. This 270-mile footpath winds along the northern backbone of England, up fells and down dales until it ends just over the Scottish border. About 6,000 intrepid hikers complete the grueling trek each year.

▲ Lincoln: Linked by river and canal to England's vast waterway system, this sleepy town set in flat, fertile farmland was once an important commercial center.

Buxton, the largest town in the area, was a fashionable spa in the 18th century. Long before that, the Romans had tested the healthful benefits of its thermal springs, and laid the foundations of the town. Among the fine buildings here is the elegant Crescent, built by the fifth Duke of Devonshire.

An earlier Duke, the fourth, was responsible for another notable building in the region. Chatsworth House, a classic Palladian mansion, is one of the great stately homes of England. Called "the Palace of

the Peak," it houses a priceless collection of paintings and sculpture, including works by Rembrandt, Van Dyck and Reynolds, as well as splendidly ornate furniture. The most spectacular of its 175 rooms are open to the public, who can also stroll through the gardens with their vast greenhouses, and explore a 1,100-acre park where herds of deer roam. The Water Garden features the Grand Cascade, a glittering staircase of water, and the 290-foot-high column of the Emperor Fountain.

Not far to the east lies Sherwood Forest, the deep, magical wood that washome of the legendary Robin Hood. With his band of Merry Men, the popular folk hero robbed from the rich and gave to the poor— and also hunted the King's deer in Sherwood's glades. Little of Sherwood Forest is left today, but trails through the woods allow visitors to explore the area, and walk in the footsteps of Robin and Maid Marian, Friar Tuck, Little John, Will Scarlet and Alan-a-Dale.

The imposing Gothic cathedral in nearby Lincoln stands on a 200-foot limestone plateau. The Romans built a camp in this strategic location; two main roads in the region follow ancient Roman routes. Lincoln Cathedral's superb stone, wood and glasswork make it one of England's greatest buildings. Perhaps its finest feature is the Angel Choir, named for the exquisitely carved figures displayed in it. The elegant library in the Cloister was built by the famous architect Sir Christopher Wren.

◄ *Lincoln: Visible from miles away, the three high towers of Lincoln Cathedral, a medieval masterpiece built of local honey-colored limestone, rise over the city and surrounding countryside.*

▲ *Compton Wyngates: This magnificent Tudor house is set in grounds populated by manicured topiary, and features several dozen corkscrew chimneys.*

Where Lincolnshire borders on the coast, the land is so low, flat and fertile that the area is called Holland. In fact, more bulbs are grown here than in its European namesake. The fields around the town of Spalding are ablaze in spring with tulips, daffodils and hyacinths.

North Americans tracing their roots to the Pilgrim Fathers often visit Boston, one of the towns where it all began. In 1607 a group of Puritans, hoping to escape religious persecution by crossing the Atlantic,

were arrested and imprisoned here. The cells in which they were held can still be seen in Boston's 15th-century Guildhall. Two decades later, another band set off for America—and this time was successful. They founded the city of Boston in the far-flung colony of Massachusetts.

Like Holland, the Fens of East Anglia, the region that protrudes in a hump on England's east coast, are fertile agriculture ground. It is believed that great forests grew here thousands of years ago, until

the trees were choked by the formation of peat. The low-lying land then flooded, and patches of high ground appeared as islands in the marsh. From the 17th century frequent attempts were made to drain the Fens, but none succeeded until Cornelius Vermuyden, a Dutch engineer, stepped in. Vermuyden's scheme involved cutting rivers through the marshes, and sluicing them against tidal inflow. Seven hundred windmills were used to pump the water into the outlets.

▲ *The rich, deep soil of South Derbyshire produces much of England's wheat and barley.*

In an astonishing feat of engineering, the fan-vaulted timber roof supports a 400-ton wooden lantern 94 feet above the floor.

North of Ely, in northern Norfolk, is Sandringham House, one of the Queen's favorite country homes. The royal family traditionally gathered here for Christmas, but now the house—which is far from small—cannot accommodate them all. When the Queen or her family is not in residence, tourists are welcome to visit the house and stroll through the surrounding rhododendron gardens and parklands. A museum on the grounds has Edward VII's sporty 1900 Daimler Tonneau, the first automobile ever purchased by a member of the royal family.

One of Norfolk's finest medieval buildings is nearby in moated Oxburgh Hall, built around 1462. A formal French garden and several finely decorated rooms are open to the public. The King's Room displays panels embroidered by Mary Queen of Scots. The Hall has been owned by one family for almost 500 years.

The charming cathedral city of Norwich has been the capital of East Anglia for ten centuries. A great port in Saxon times, it went on to become a center of the wool trade, then moved into banking, engineering and shoemaking.

► Norfolk: Linked with a series of rivers, lakes and streams, the manmade channels called the Broads offer boating enthusiasts some 200 miles of waterways.

Yet Norwich has retained a sense of history. Its cobblestoned streets are lined by ancient timber-framed shops, some dating from the 14th century. The sturdy Norman keep of Norwich Castle, on a huge mound in the city center, was once the county jail. It now houses an impressive museum, displaying paintings by artists of the Norwich school and dioramas of Norfolk wildlife, complete with an enchanting recording of local birdsong. Norwich Cathedral, with its huge Norman nave and tower, dates back to 1096. Soaring 315 feet towards the sky and dominating the city is an elegant, tapering spire that was added in the 15th century.

The principle remains the same today, except that diesel and electric pumps have replaced the windmills.

Ely means "Eel Island," for the town is built on a hummock of land that was once an island before the Fens were drained. Massive Ely Cathedral, with its unique octagonal lantern tower rising high above the town's rooftops, is truly a magnificent sight. In 1322 carpenters searched throughout England for oak trees large enough to act as the tower's corner posts.

▲ Near Swaffham: The most striking architectural feature of moated Oxburgh Hall is its Tudor gatehouse, with 80-foot octagonal twin towers above the bridge.

► Ely: "Queen of the Fens," Ely Cathedral can be seen for miles around. At 248 feet, the nave is one of the longest in England; its wooden ceiling is 72 feet high.

Not far from Norwich, a series of channels called the Norfolk Broads offer boating enthusiasts some 200 miles of navigable water. At one time it was thought that the Broads were natural formations, but recent evidence has shown them to be the result of medieval peat-digging. Visitors can rent motorboats to meander along these peaceful waterways, glimpsing a family of swans or a lonely heron among the reeds, or stopping for a pint at a waterside pub. Thatched cottages at their best can be seen along the Broads. At one time a dying art, the craft has been revived, and collecting reeds for thatching is a profitable business hereabouts. Each artisan lays and cuts the reeds to produce his own distinctive pattern.

In Suffolk County to the south, the town of Bury St. Edmunds bills itself as "Shrine of a King, Cradle of the Law." The "king" is St. Edmund, an East Anglian monarch murdered in 869 and later canonized and buried here. The "law" refers to the group of barons who, in 1214, vowed before St. Edmund's shrine that they would force King John to sign that immortal document, the Magna Carta.

Many of the town's older houses, some dating from the 12th century, hide behind Georgian façades. And like many places in England, Bury St. Edmunds has been immortalized in the writings of Charles Dickens. The great novelist had his character Mr. Pickwick stay at the Angel Hotel; he was here when he learned of a breach of promise suit filed against him. The Nutshell, a Victorian drinking establishment, claims the dubious distinction of being the smallest pub in England.

Southern Suffolk is Constable country, for it is here that the great painter was born, and these landscapes that inspired his art. His birthplace at East Bergholt lies near the banks of the River Stour. The valley has changed little since the days when the young artist's eye was enchanted by the millwheels and locks along the river, and the leafy trees that shaded its waters. "I associate my careless boyhood with all that lies on the banks of the Stour," wrote the artist, "those scenes made me a painter."

The university town of Cambridge to the west has spawned some of the world's greatest philosophers, scientists and poets. It was in the 13th century that scholars began gathering here; the first college was founded in 1284. As the university thrived, scores of buildings sprang up. The finest is King's College Chapel, considered by many the most beautiful Gothic building in Europe. Its soaring stone spires, magnificent fan-vaulting and 16th-century stained-glass windows portraying scenes from the New Testament delight the eye. A jewel within a jewel, the Rubens painting "Adoration of the Magi" forms the chapel's altar-piece. Every Christmas Eve, the chapel reverberates with music as the world-famous choir sings carols that are broadcast around the world.

The River Cam flows through Cambridge, and the broad lawns of the colleges that slope down to its banks are called the "Backs." Though parts of the university are closed to tourists, anyone can rent a punt and drift beneath the willows for fine views of the Backs. In fact, some parts of Cambridge are best seen from the Cam, especially the enclosed bridge over the river at St. John's College. Known as the Bridge of Sighs, it was modeled after a 16th-century counterpart in Venice.

▲ *Cambridge: The ingenious Mathematicians' Bridge was built in 1749 without a single nail. A curious Victorian who dismantled it in 1867 couldn't reassemble it without iron bolts.*

▲ *Cambridge: Seen from the River Cam, the glorious towers of King's College Chapel, one of the supreme achievements of Gothic architecture, dominate the other buildings of the college.*

► *Cambridge: Emblazoned with a Tudor coat of arms and heraldic carvings and topped with turrets, a massive gatehouse leads into the splendors of St. John's College.*

Castles
and Coal

The natural resources in England's northeastern counties of Northumberland, Durham and Yorkshire brought them a key role in the Industrial Revolution. Yet despite the development of the region's rich deposits of coal and iron ore, the wild hills here frame some of the country's largest tracts of unspoiled countryside. The massive Pennine mountain range stretches the full length of the northeast corner, and glaciers flowing from its lofty peaks have carved a dramatic landscape of limestone cliffs and valleys in the Yorkshire Dales.

York is the great city of this region. To step through one of its four medieval gates is to relive history. Ancient alleyways such as the Shambles, the former butchers' quarter, have hardly changed for centuries. Some of the lanes are so narrow that the overhanging second stories of the houses almost touch those of the row across the street.

The city's imaginative Castle Museum, housed in a former 18th-century prison, brings the past to life. Here a cobblestoned street with reconstructed storefronts and hansom cabs recreates Victorian times; other displays show life from Tudor to Edwardian days. The Jorvik Viking Centre takes visitors even farther back in time, to the sights, sounds and even smells of a 10th-century Viking village.

◄ York: The towers of York Minster, England's largest medieval cathedral, rise above the walls of this ancient city. Its stained-glass windows are among country's greatest art treasures.

▲ *Near Richmond: The broadest and most open of the Yorkshire valleys, Wensleydale is famous for its sheep and cheese. Seven hundred square miles of the Dales form a national park.*

Not far to the northeast of York, treasure-filled Castle Howard was begun in 1700 as the baroque home of the earls of Carlisle. The mansion and 10,000 acres of parkland surrounding it recently gained widespread admiration when they appeared as a backdrop for the television production of Evelyn Waugh's *Brideshead Revisited.*

The thriving market town of Thirsk has also attracted attention for its literary connections. Yorkshire is James Herriot country, and the famous author/veterinarian has made Thirsk into the "Harrowby" of his charming animal stories. In fact, despite his overwhelming success as a writer, Herriot still maintains a practice here.

For thousands of years sheep have grazed the Yorkshire moors, making this a major wool-producing region. Leeds, Yorkshire's largest city, is an important industrial center, producing much woollen ready-made clothing and a wide range of other manufactured items. Just west of Leeds lies the little town of Haworth, home of the famous Brontë family. The parsonage where the sisters lived is now a museum; the pub where their brother, Branwell, drank himself to death still stands. It was on the bleak, melancholy moors near here that Heathcliff mourned his Cathy; and a ruined farm at High Withens is believed to have been the inspiration for *Wuthering Heights.*

The rolling hills of Yorkshire come to an abrupt stop at Whitby, a picturesque fishing port and seaside resort. The explorer Captain James Cook lived in Whitby, and learned the seafaring craft abord Whitby boats. The crumbling sandstone remains

▲ *Spurn Head: A favorite stopover for migrating birds, this sliver of land at the mouth of the Humber River provides a welcome sanctuary for wild swans and other waterfowl.*

of 13th-century Whitby Abbey stand on a high headland above the town, an imposing sight which inspired Bram Stoker's work, *Dracula.* Stoker had the ship carrying the dreaded vampire drift ashore at Whitby; the black dog that bounded from it was Count Dracula in disguise.

At one time, England's northeast corner was frontier country, and inhabitants here had to defend themselves against marauding Scottish lords. The closer the castles and great houses in this region are to the Scottish border, the heavier their fortifications. The university city of Durham has the only castle in the north country never to have fallen to the invading Scots. Durham's superb cathedral is said to be the finest Norman building in the world.

Today new housing and development are replacing the soot and grime that once characterized Newcastle upon Tyne.

changed for the better since then. In 1952 Manchester was the first city to follow England's new "smokeless zone" regulations; today more than 26 square miles in this region comply with the antipollution laws. Slums have been cleared, buildings once soot-laden now gleam and the slag heaps from neighboring coal mines have been broken down to form the foundations for the expressway.

But people in the crowded cities of the North still need some breathing space, and they find it in the coastal towns that have been dubbed "the lungs of Lancashire." The best beaches and swimming can be had at the lively resorts of Blackpool and Lytham St. Anne's. Frequent ferries from here take visitors to the Isle of Man, set in the Irish Sea midway between England and Ireland. The island is known for its mild climate, lonely walks, and the tailless cats first bred here some 300 years ago. Because of their large hindquarters, legend has it that the Manx is actually a cross between a cat and a hare.

The compact Lake District contains what is arguably the finest scenery in England. Here hillsides bright with bluebells slope gently down toward placid waters; Herdwick sheep graze in meadows bordered by ancient stone walls; picturesque cottages nestle at the foot of towering peaks. This jewel set amidst the Cumbrian Mountains has only 16 lakes, ranging in size from Windermere, at ten miles long, to tiny Brothers Water, less than half a mile. In 1951 the Lake District was designated a national park. Despite its popularity, the countryside has remained relatively unspoiled since the days when Wordsworth wrote:

I wandered lonely as a cloud
That floats on high o'er vales and hills,
When all at once I saw a crowd,
A host, of golden daffodils.

Each spring, the hillsides near the towns of Grasmere and Rydal Mount, where Wordsworth made his homes, are still golden with daffodils. Dove Cottage, where the poet lived from 1799 to 1808, is open to the public; a museum nearby displays manuscripts, portraits and mementos of Wordsworth and fellow writers who visited him here: Sir Walter Scott, Charles Lamb and Samuel Taylor Coleridge.

The Lake District is a favorite with walkers, for new vistas seem to open up with every step. Many visitors make the town of Ambleside their headquarters, staying at comfortable bed-and-breakfast inns and exploring the surrounding fells along well-marked footpaths. A hike to the sum-

At one time this bustling city was no more than a minor fort at one end of Hadrian's Wall. The ruins of this ancient fortification are Britain's most spectacular reminder of the Roman occupation. The mighty wall, originally some 15 feet high, was begun by Roman soldiers in the second century as a defense against Scottish marauders. It stretched 73 miles across northern England, and took eight years to build. Remaining portions of the wall snake for miles across the spine of Britain, dotted by the ruins of forts, Roman mile castles and signal towers.

One of the best collections of Roman antiquities in England is in the town of Chester, on the western coast opposite South Yorkshire. The Romans established a camp here in A.D. 79, and many of the enclosing ramparts built by them are standing to this day. An ancient Roman amphitheatre has been partially excavated just outside the city walls.

Before gaining fame as the home of the Beatles, Liverpool was a thriving Atlantic seaport with seven miles of waterfront, two modern cathedrals, a respected university and a number of artists, writers and entertainers who have had a lasting effect on British culture. To capitalize on its most famous sons, Liverpool offers Beatle City, with its impressive display of John, Paul, George and Ringo memorabilia and souvenirs. The Cavern Mecca, another museum, features a full-size replica of the club where many Liverpudlians heard history in the making as the Beatles played their first dates.

"Festering in planless chaos" is how George Orwell once described the luckless city of Manchester. Happily, this major industrial center in northwest England has

▲ *Whitby: A gaunt shell, Whitby Abbey inspired the author of Dracula. The building owes its ruined condition to the ravages of time—and a 1914 shelling by the German fleet.*

► *Wasdale Head: From this starting point, lines of climbers set off to pick their way up the boulder-strewn flanks of Scafell Pike, England's highest point.*

mit of 3,210-foot Scafell Pike is a more strenuous undertaking, but a safe one providing climbers keep to the recognized routes. (Several rock-climbers killed on the surrounding peaks are buried in the tiny churchyard of nearby Wasdale Head.) The breathtaking view from the top takes in the lakes of Windermere, Derwent Water, and Wast Water, England's deepest.

The tranquil village of Near Sawrey on the west side of Lake Windermere was home to Beatrix Potter, the beloved author of *The Tale of Peter Rabbit*. She used her house, Hill Top, as the setting for her stories; the mice, rabbits, cats and ducks that lived here modeled for her charming illustrations.

► *Chester: This town's unique architectural feature is The Rows, double tiers of shops that open onto balustraded galleries. The oldest date from 1486.*

SCOTLAND

With its lonely moors and wild, silent mountain passes, Scotland is one of the last great wilderness areas in Europe. To most North Americans, Scotland may seem small geographically—its total land area is no bigger than the state of Maine—but the country and its people have left a powerful legacy. Scotland's turbulent history, with its cast of romantic heroes and heroines, is dear to the heart of every Scot.

For centuries Scotland was a nest of warring tribes fighting a bitter struggle to maintain its independence from England. That struggle ended in 1603, when Scotland's James VI became James I of England, succeeding Elizabeth I. In 1707, to the bitter and enduring resentment of many Scots, the parliaments of Scotland and England were united.

To this day Scottish law is different from that of England, and Scotland retains her own Church and institutions. Most Scots see themselves as stubbornly separate from the rest of Britain. Many visitors who come here hope to celebrate that difference, and discover the Scottish roots laid down by their families generations ago.

Scotland is divided into two parts, the southern half, called the Lowlands, and the northern half, called the Highlands. The Lowlands are largely made up of heather-clad plateaus, grassy pasture land and green dales. Most of the population is here, as are Scotland's two largest cities, Glasgow and Edinburgh. The more sparsely populated Highlands have Britain's loftiest mountains, slashed by gorges with foaming waterfalls; as well as lonely lochs and windswept islands.

▲ *Prodigious lung power is required to play them, but no Scottish celebration is complete without the skirl of the bagpipes.*

◄ *Buttermere Lake: A footpath that leads all the way around this jewel-like lake winds past pine trees and bracken, and at one point threads through a tunnel in a cliff.*

▲ *Glencoe: In this infamous valley in 1692, a shocking incident of clan warfare took place, Campbells massacring MacDonalds. A monument to the murdered chief stands near the glen.*

The Bonnie Lowlands

For centuries the area where Scotland meets England, called the Borders, was a battlefield between the warring English and Scots. The gutted abbeys that can still be seen in Jedburgh, Melrose, Kelso and Dryburgh were destroyed by English invaders between the 13th and 17th centuries. The region's inhabitants also lived in constant fear of Border bandits, who terrorized local villages.

This long history of violence, coupled with the beauty and romance of the countryside, inspired the writer Sir Walter Scott. Descended from Border people, Scott was born in 1771 in Edinburgh but spent much of his adult life at Abbotsford House, his home near the Border town of Melrose. Scott's romantic novels brought Scotland's tempestuous history back to life, and made him the most successful writer of his day.

Abbotsford, Scott's handsome house overlooking the River Tweed, is open to the public. Besides a large collection of Scott memorabilia, there are displays of weapons and armor used in the Border wars. The ghostly ruins of Melrose Abbey, thought to be among the finest in Scotland, sparked Scott's imagination. In *The Lay of the Last Minstrel* he wrote: "If thou would see fair Melrose aright/Go visit it by the pale moonlight."

The thousands of sheep grazing along the River Tweed provide the wool that keeps a major local industry alive. For two centuries the rough, warm fabric called tweed has been woven in the Borderlands, and exported around the world. Scottish wool is also woven into the famous tartans—plaids whose colors and patterns indicate the wearer's clan. Though it's generally believed that most tartans are centuries old, in fact many date only from the 19th century, when Scott's novels created a vogue for things Scottish.

Vast farms mark the region around North Berwick on the east coast. Many large houses in the area have unusual dovecotes on their grounds—relics of the Middle Ages, when pigeons were kept for food. Sandy beaches at North Berwick make this town a popular seaside resort. As is the case almost everywhere in Scotland, people spend much of their leisure

time on golf courses. This part of Scotland has been called "The Holy Land of Golf;" enthusiasts here have been playing the game since the 16th century.

Farther east the shoreline becomes rocky and precipitous, providing a dramatic site for the ruins of Dunbar Castle, destroyed during Cromwell's campaign to subdue the Scots in 1650. Nearly 3,000 valiant Scots were killed in one day during the Battle of Dunbar. Down the coast, Fast Castle is immortalized as "Wolf's Crag" in Scott's *The Bride of Lammermoor.*

Edinburgh Castle, the crowning glory of Scotland's capital city, has fared better. Its rooms and relics tell the story of Scotland's colorful past. Tiny St. Margaret's Chapel is the oldest building in Edinburgh. It dates from around 1100, and has survived many perils. In a room in the Royal Palace, Mary Queen of Scots gave birth to James VI, who was to become James I of England. The Crown Chamber houses the 14th-century Honours of Scotland—the Scottish Crown Jewels.

The Royal Mile is the name given to a row of ancient streets leading from the Castle down to the Royal Palace of Holyroodhouse. It owes its unusual architecture to the Flodden Wall, built after 1513 to protect the people of Edinburgh against attacks by the English. For some 250 years, Edinburgh citizens lived in such fear that they refused to build outside the wall. As a result, the city grew up, not out.

Today Edinburgh is a safe, clean, vibrant city, but in medieval days citizens in that warren of dark, malodorous housing suffered from chronic water shortage and a nonexistent sewage system. Though the 1707 Act of Union was anathema to many

Scots, it gave Edinburgh a new lease on life. Freed of the danger of invasion, the city could at last break out of its ancient walls and expand.

Edinburgh's New Town, the section that sprang up in the 18th century, has been called "the most extensive example of a Romantic Classical city in the world. Princes Street and Queen Street are a tribute to the foresight of city planner James Craig, who directed that one side of each street should be made up of elegant Georgian facades; the other side devoted to public gardens. A feature of the West Princes Street Gardens is the world's oldest floral clock, built in 1903.

Edinburgh owes its nickname of "the Athens of the North" to several unusual structures. In 1829 the Royal High School was modeled after the Temple of Theseus in Athens; it is now an art center. A monument to Scots killed in the Napoleonic Wars which stands proudly on a hill above the city was meant to reproduce the Parthenon, but a lack of funds intervened before its completion.

From Edinburgh, a bridge leads across the Firth of Forth ("firth" means estuary) to the Kingdom of Fife, the hunting retreat

▲ *In a Scottish show of strength, a Highlander prepares to toss the caber, a 132-pound log that must turn end over end before it lands.*

▲ *Edinburgh: Kilts mingle with jeans before the Gothic portals of St. Giles's Cathedral in the Royal Mile. In the 16th century, John Knox preached his fiery Calvinism from its pulpit.*

► *Kyle of Lochalsh: Deep, fjord-like "kyles" carve up Scotland's rugged west coast. Car ferries leave here regularly for the five-minute hop to the Isle of Skye.*

of the Stuart monarchs. The picturesque coastline with its string of unspoiled fishing villages is known as East Neuk. Dunfermline, a busy textile-producing town and the birthplace of industrialist Andrew Carnegie, was earlier the home of Scottish kings from the 11th century until 1603. Seven of them, including King Robert the Bruce, are buried there.

Most Scots scoff at the legend that golf was brought here by Dutch traders. In any case, the game was perfected in the sand traps, fields and hedgerows of St. Andrews. Golfers have cursed and exulted their way through the 18 holes of the famous Old Course for around 800 years. The grandly named Royal and Ancient Golf Club, founded here in 1754, is the world's ruling authority on golf.

At the mouth of the River Clyde stands Scotland's largest city, Glasgow. Often scorned by tourists, Glasgow earned its reputation from grimy factories, crime-ridden docks and centuries-old slums. Today Glasgow is undergoing a renaissance. Heavy industries such as shipbuilding and iron and steel works have declined,

new housing developments are replacing overcrowded slums, and stringent antipollution regulations are cleaning up the air. Glasgow is now the home of the arts in Scotland, boasting the country's only opera house, two orchestras, and some of the finest art collections in Britain.

The famous bonnie, bonnie banks of Loch Lomond lie only a few miles to the north. A 23-mile lake studded with islands and ringed by hills and mountains, it has been a favorite tourist destination for nearly two centuries. The nostalgic song "Loch Lomond" is said to have been composed by a follower of Bonnie Prince Charlie. Awaiting execution, he sings about the "low road" his spirit will take to return to his beloved homeland.

Nearby Bannockburn was the site of a decisive battle in 1314, when Robert the Bruce routed an English army three times larger than his own, thus securing Scotland's independence. This battlefield, where Scotland's greatest victory over the English took place, is dear to the hearts of all Scotsmen. The declaration of Arbroath, which Robert the Bruce signed in 1320, testifies: "For so long as a hundred of us are left alive, we will yield in no least way to English dominion."

West of Glasgow is the region called Argyll, which takes in a dramatic coastline of islands, inlets and peninsulas. Along the lochs and seacoast, the terraced gardens of holiday villages slope down toward the water. Frequent ferry trips take visitors to Glasgow's favorite playground, delightful Arran Island. Called "Scotland in miniature," Arran has its own small mountains, lochs, streams, moors and glens, as well as Bronze Age cairns, a castle built in 1456, and three sheltered bays.

Several of the other islands here are also popular vacation spots, as is the long peninsula called the Mull of Kintyre (celebrated in Paul McCartney's song of the same name—the former Beatle keeps a home here). In the mild climate, subtropical gardens thrive, seals bask on the sea rocks and the pace of living is gentle. Despite this bucolic atmosphere, it was on the island of Jura that Orwell penned his bleak prophesy, the novel *1984*.

The land of Scotland's national poet, Robert Burns, lies farther down the coast at Ayrshire. Burns was born at Alloway, in a thatched cottage that is now a museum. The countryside is rife with places immortalized in Burns' poems: bridges called "the Auld Brig o' Ayr" and the "Brig o' Doon," the Tam o' Shanter Inn and Souter (cobbler) Johnnie's cottage.

The first edition of Burns' poems was published in Kilmarnock, a town which also has connections with another famous Scotsman: Johnny Walker. More than just a name on a label, Walker started blending whiskey here in 1820; the whiskey-bottling company he founded is now the largest in the world. A number of factors give Scotch whiskey its distinctive taste: Scotland's clear, soft water; its pure air and cold climate; fine barley; fragrant peat smoke; and distilling techniques passed down over centuries.

Eastward along the coast lies Dumfries, a quaint town called "The Queen of the South." Like Ayr, Dumfries is thronged with Burns fans in summer, come to visit the town where the Ploughman Poet spent the last of his 37 years. The Globe Inn, his favorite howff (an old Scottish expression for pub), is little changed from the days when Burns drank and flirted with the barmaid here (the flirting worked—she bore him a child). The quaint stone house in which Burns lived is now a museum; an elaborate mausoleum in nearby St. Michael's Churchyard is the final resting place of Scotland' favorite son.

Strategically placed Gretna Green lies just over the border from England. Until 1856, lovers forbidden by English law to marry in England could cross the border and tie the knot in Scotland. Many star-crossed couples landed in Gretna Green, where Scots law required only witnesses, and no ceremony, for a wedding. The village blacksmith usually did the honors, until a killjoy law passed in 1856 required one member of the couple to reside in Scotland for three weeks.

▲ *Edinburgh: Above the rose gardens that perfume the air along Princes Street looms Edinburgh Castle, perched on a rock believed to an extinct volcano.*

▲ *Small, shaggy Highland cattle are a hardy native breed that thrives on Scotland's moors. Lacking productive arable land, the country earns most of its farm income from livestock.*

▲ *Near Scourie: Miniature islands dot the coastline of the far northwest. This sparsely populated region has fewer than seven people to the square mile.*

A Highland Fling

Visitors who come to Scotland looking for spectacular scenery in a wild, solitary setting invariably head north for the Highlands and Islands. Here are purple heather and wooded glens, great inland lochs fed by clear, icy streams, and snowy peaks that yield panoramic views at every turn.

Athough the Scottish Highlands cover about a quarter of Britain's total land surface, it is home to less than two percent of its population. Yet many parts of the Highlands have known the hand of man—then fallen again into wilderness. Ruins of castles recall the turmoil of the Middle Ages. Crumbling cottages are a reminder of the Clearances, when landowners in the late 18th and early 19th centuries cruelly evicted tenants to make way for sheep. Another wave of Highlanders was forced out by London-based aristocrats wanting to create their own private shooting and fishing preserves, such as that of Queen Victoria at Balmoral.

Today the government seeking to populate Scotland's northern regions with tourists, and to capitalize on the North Sea oil boom that began to bring new prosperity in the early 1970s. But Scotland's most lonely regions are still a haven to those weary of city life.

Off the west coast, the magic islands of the Inner Hebrides offer a wealth of wildlife and a history rich in ghosts, monsters and fairies. The wild scenery of the Isle of Mull figured largely in Robert Louis Stevenson's *Kidnapped*. Thirteenth-century Duart Castle on a crag overlooking the east coast is the ancestral home of the chiefs of the Clan Maclean. By the 20th century it had fallen into disrepair, but Sir Fitzroy Maclean undertook to restore it in 1911, and his grandson, the present chief of the clan, lives there today.

A ferry from Mull takes passengers to the enchanting islet of Iona. For centuries Iona has been known as a place of spiritual power. It was here that an Irish nobleman first brought Christianity to Scotland by establishing an abbey in A.D. 563. The island is also famous for the "Graves of the Kings." From the sixth century, a total of 59 kings were buried here, including both Macbeth and his victim, Duncan.

The jagged coastline of north Argyll, on the mainland, offers motorists miles of breathtaking seascapes. Glencoe, also called the Glen of Weeping, is the site of the most brutal massacre in the history of Scotland. In 1692, in this narrow, seven-mile valley, a company of 200 soldiers commanded by Robert Campbell turned on some 40 MacDonalds who had hospitably sheltered them for 12 days, and slaughtered men, women and children. The English King William III was said to have ordered the bloodbath, supposedly

to punish the MacDonald chief for his reluctance to swear allegiance to the King of England. Whatever the reason, Glencoe lives on as a reminder; and to this day there is no love lost between the Mac-Donalds and Campbells.

Farther inland is a strip of land, no more than five miles wide, that has been called "the Highlands in Miniature." The Trossachs (the word means "bristly country")

▲ It takes plenty of Highland sheep to produce the wool for fine Scottish tartans. A single kilt requires seven to ten yards of woven fabric.

▲ A'hunting he will go: Sportsmen from all over the world come to northern Scotland to shoot red grouse, woodcock and capercaillie, or to stalk red deer. All hunting is done on private land.

offer compact views of some mountains, streams, moors and glens bordered by lovely lochs. Sir Walter Scott set his poem "The Lady of the Lake" on Loch Katrine in the Trossachs; he also immortalized Rob Roy, an historical figure here. Local opinion was divided on Rob Roy. Some saw him as a sort of Scottish Robin Hood, others as no more than a common bandit and cattle thief.

"Amid all the provinces of Scotland," wrote Sir Walter Scott in his 1828 novel, *The Fair Maid of Perth*, "if an intelligent stranger were asked to describe the most varied and most beautiful, it is probable he would name the county of Perth." Scott's judgment still holds true, for this county offers lush farmlands, the best of beautiful Scottish scenery, along with medieval castles and acres of golf courses.

The town of Scone used to be the coronation place of Scottish kings. The ceremony took place on the "Stone of Destiny," also called the Stone of Scone, said to have been brought here in the ninth century by Kenneth MacAlpin, the first King of the Scots and Picts. In 1297 Edward I took the coveted piece of granite to London; today it resides beneath the Coronation Chair in Westminster Abbey.

▲ *Glencoe: The bald mountains that surround the seven-mile valley make the area a favorite among experienced rock climbers.*

Productive farms thrive in the fertile Vale of Strathmore northeast of Perth, specializing in a championship breed of beef cattle—the hornless, black Aberdeen Angus. Vast herds can be seen from the battlements of Glamis Castle, a house that has had royal connections for ten centuries. The Earls of Strathmore have been lairds of Glamis for 500 years; the Queen Mother, daughter of the Earl of Strathmore, was raised here. This is where Queen Elizabeth II spent much of her childhood, and where Princess Margaret was born the first royal princess to be born in Scotland in three centuries. The castle, built mainly in the style of a 17th-century French chateau, is said to harbor no less than nine ghosts, as well as a monster believed to have been bricked up in a secret chamber 200 years ago. The otherworldly residents have been known to make the odd surprise appearance.

Dundee, a seaport on the Firth of Tay, is also known as the town of jam, jute and journalism. The flourishing jam industry began with Mrs. Keiller's marmalade in 1797; today it processes much of the fruit grown in the region. The jute trade grew as a by-product of the local whaling industry, when seamen discovered that raw jute imported from India could be mixed with whale oil, then woven into the coarse fabric used for mats and bags. And the Dundee publisher D.C. Thompson produces newspapers, weeklies and books read throughout Britain.

The east-coast city of Aberdeen has long been known for its activity in the shipping trade. In the mid-19th century, Aberdeen clippers raced the wind to bring their valuable cargoes of tea from China; the fishing fleet kept the mile of dockside sheds so busy that they filled and emptied three times with a single day's catch. But until

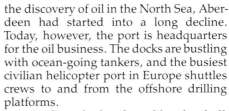

the discovery of oil in the North Sea, Aberdeen had started into a long decline. Today, however, the port is headquarters for the oil business. The docks are bustling with ocean-going tankers, and the busiest civilian helicopter port in Europe shuttles crews to and from the offshore drilling platforms.

Away from the hustle and bustle of offshore oil, the area around Aberdeen is rich in one of Scotland's greatest commodities: castles. Some are seemingly impregnable stone fortresses, others delicate, turreted structures straight from a book of fairy tales. Crathes Castle has magnificent painted ceilings and lovely gardens; 14th-century Kildrummy Castle has an imaginative Alpine garden planted by Japanese landscape architects in 1904. It is easy to imagine Rapunzel letting down her hair from the towers of Craigievar, with their high gables and conical roofs.

▲ *Orkney Islands: Guarding the ragged coastline of the island of Hoy is the "Old Man of Hoy," a strange, columnar rock formation. Its 450-foot height was climbed for the first time in 1966.*

Balmoral Castle is open to the public only between May and July, for this is the royal family's summer home. It was bought by Queen Victoria and Prince Albert in 1853, and rebuilt in the Scottish baronial style. Queen Elizabeth usually tries to schedule her visit to Balmoral for late August or early September, to allow her to attend the world-renowned Royal Highland Gathering, held six miles from Balmoral in the town of Braemar. Each year Highlanders gather to engage in such sports as caber tossing, hammer throwing, tug-o'-wars and relay races. Highland dancing and sword-dancing competitions are accompanied by the wail of bagpipes.

West of Aberdeen the land rises into the rugged Cairngorm and northern Grampian mountains. This is Scotland's winter sports capital, with the best skiing in all of Britain. Aviemore, at the region's center, was transformed in the 1960s into an af-

fluent, year-round holiday resort, offering ski hills, ice-skating and curling in winter; sailing, canoeing, mountain climbing and the ubiquitous golf in summer.

Scotland is not known for its balmy climate, so the expression "Scottish Riviera" may seem contradictory. But the mild climate along the Morae coast does compare favorably with that of the rest of Scotland. The water temperature, alas, is many degrees cooler than its Mediteranean counterpart. Anyone tempted to take a dip, however, would find just the remedy along the nearby Whiskey Trail. This 70-mile tour runs through the glens of Speyside. Half of Scotland's malt distilleries lie here along the Spey River valley, since the peat streams that flow from the Grampian Hills into the Spey provide the water that makes Highland single-malt whiskey unique. Several distilleries, including Glenlivet and Glenfiddich, offer

guided tours and even a wee dram of their *uisge beatha* — the "water of life."

The town of Inverness is known as the "Capital of the Highlands." The "modern" Inverness Castle dates only from 1835; it stands on the site of a fortress that was blown up by the Jacobites in 1746. The town's most significant historic site is at Culloden, five miles east. It was on Culloden's bleak moor, on April 16, 1746, that Bonnie Prince Charlie and his army of 5,000 Highlanders met the English army, led by the Duke of Cumberland. Within 40 minutes, 1,200 Highlanders lay dead. For his part in the massacre, the Duke of Cumberland earned the name "Butcher Cumberland" among the Scots. Although Bonnie Prince Charlie escaped with his life, the bitter defeat meant an end to the Stuart line. At Culloden, communal burial sites are marked by simple headstones bearing the names of the various clans

▲ *Shetland Islands: Tiny villages dot the coast line of these windswept isles, which lie at the center of rich fishing grounds. No point on the islands is more than three miles from the sea.*

► *Eilean Donnan Castle: Despite its remote site deep in the heart of northern Scotland, this majestic castle has long been a favorite Scottish subject for painters and photographers.*

names of the various clans who took part.

Northwest of Inverness, some of Scotland's few remaining indigenous wild animals still roam the wild glens and forests: the diminutive red deer; shy, bushy-tailed Scottish wildcats; otters, pine martens, osprey and golden eagles. Most of these are difficult to spot, but it's even harder to catch a glimpse of Scotland's most renowned indigenous beast: the Loch Ness Monster. Though there is no unequivocal proof of her existence, "Nessie" has been sighted by many. Locals capitalize on the monster's noteriety by selling everything from t-shirts to "Nessie burgers."

On the west coast, the busy shipping village called Kyle of Lochalsh is a departure point for ferry trips to the Isle of Skye. Perhaps the loveliest of all the Scottish islands, Skye is mountainous and mystical,

a land of lingering sunsets, soft mists and romantic legends. Bonnie Prince Charlie fled to the Isle of Skye after the Battle of Culloden; Flora MacDonald, the woman who helped him escape by disguising him as her maid, is buried on the island. Dunvegan Castle on the west coast is thought to be the oldest inhabited castle in Britain. For 700 years it has been the seat of the Clan MacLeod.

Beyond Skye lie the sea-worn Outer Hebrides, a 130-mile string of rugged, treeless islands. The inhabitants of the tiny villages are warm, sociable people whose first language is Gaelic. Tourism is their main source of income, but many work at fishing, crofting, or weaving the famous Harris tweed. In these northerly climes, daylight may linger for 18 hours in late spring, and the light reflected from

the sea gives the islands a luminous quality that draws artists and photographers.

The windswept Orkneys and Shetlands lie to the north of the Scottish mainland, a path of stepping-stones that includes 165 islands. Brightly painted cottages cluster in tiny, sheltered villages, and coastal cliffs are alive with gulls, cormorants, petrels, puffins and gannets. Orkney's two main towns—Stromness and Kirkwall—have narrow, cobblestoned streets and charming historic buildings. On the Shetland Islands, thousands of acres are reserved for the small sheep whose wool goes to the famous Shetland sweaters. Despite changes brought by the North Sea oil boom—newly constructed oil terminals, busy helicopter ports—life in these isolated isles goes on much the same as it has for centuries.

▲ *Near Helmsdale: Cattle graze along the North Sea coast near the Scotland's northern tip. Much of the land here has been uninhabited since crofters were evicted in the Clearances.*

► *Glamis: Perhaps the nine ghosts said to haunt turreted Glamis Castle inspired Shakespeare to name Macbeth the "Thane of Glamis·" The castle was the childhood home of the Queen Mother.*

WALES

Even today there is no better way to insult a Welshman than to call him English. The Welsh have enduring memories, and the story of their centuries-old struggle for independence is still clear in their minds. Though both England and Wales have been administered by the same rulers in London since 1536, the Welsh cling tenaciously to their unique traditions, culture, language and way of life. About a fifth of the population speaks Welsh as naturally as they do English, and some 32,000 people in remote areas speak no English at all.

This tiny country, scarcely bigger than the state of New Jersey, is a land rich in music, magic and poetry. Its rugged beauty reveals itself in the steep slopes of some of the highest peaks in Great Britain, and in the wild grandeur of its woods and moorlands. Hereford cattle and Welsh Black sheep graze on rolling pastures, and along the coast dramatic headlands carved by the sea abound with birds.

Though there is no radical change in landscape as one passes from England into Wales, the distinction between the two is unmistakable. Road signs are in English and Welsh; but there are also more subtle differences, in the buildings, villages, even in the attitude of the people.

The county of Powys, which stretches along the border through central Wales, abounds in both wildlife and history. The population in the northern part is small and scattered; in the hedgerows and woods of the countryside thrive foxes, badgers, pine martens and red kites.

▲ *Cardiff: In the late 19th century, the owner of Cardiff Castle transformed the interior into a Victorian extravaganza. Throughout the year, medieval banquets are held here for the public.*

Residents of lovely Machynlleth in the Dyfi ("Dovey" in English) Valley are proud of the role their town once played in the struggle for Welsh independence. A parliament held here in 1404 proclaimed patriot Owen Glendower king of Wales; Machynlleth was named the capital, a privilege the town enjoyed for only a short time. The Senate House, a stone building where Glendower held his first assembly, can still be seen.

Nearby Newtown is famous as the birthplace of a pioneer of socialism, Robert Owen. Appalled by the inhuman working conditions in factories, he became an ardent campaigner for their reform. Born in Newtown in 1771, he traveled extensively throughout Britain and the United States sharing his philosophy, and returned to Newtown to die in 1858.

The old black-and-white, half-timbered houses in Welshpool to the north are typical of this area. An important market town since 1263, Welshpool swarms with livestock dealers every Monday. Hundreds of sheep and cattle are trucked in from the border towns of England and Wales to be auctioned off. Just outside town is stately Powys Castle, one of the most beautiful and well-preserved string of the great castles built in the 13th century. Its formal gardens, laid out in the dutch style around 1690, have survived 300 years of changing fashions.

In Central Powys to the south, a once-famous spa is now a resort town devoted to physical exercise. The mineral waters of Llandrindod Wells made it a mecca for the wealthy and over-indulgent in Victorian and Edwardian days, when gout was a fashionable complaint. The town's wide streets and spacious Victorian buildings now accommodate holidayers who come to enjoy the local golf, fishing and boating. Another sport enjoyed here is toad-watching. Each spring, the local toad population travels from the woods to a nearby lake, and local toad-lovers erect warning signs ("Migratory Toad Crossing") to detour traffic around them.

Brecon in south Powys is the main base for exploring the hills and valleys of nearby Brecon Beacons National Park. The park's name comes from the "Beacons," windswept peaks once used as sites for signal fires. The highest point is Peny Fan at 2,906 feet; its top can be reached in

about an hour of climbing. Rivers have carved immense caves that extend for 20 miles, decorated with stalagmites and stalactites, under the Black Mountains.

Most of the inhabitants of Powys county are farmers, but toward the south the occupations change to mining and industry. Part of Gwent County lies on the South Wales coalfield, developed in the last century. As towns sprang up in the steep valleys, tightly packed rows of terraced houses had to be built to accommodate the miners and their families. Both living and working conditions became intolerable, and social unrest resulted.

Most of the mines have since closed down. The local housing, still cramped, has been spruced up, and a major reclamation program is aimed at reforesting the hills blighted by industry, purifying the streams, and turning the country's numerous narrow-gauge railways and canals into tourist attractions.

This part of Wales is border country, and here the Normans put up dozens of military strongholds in an effort to maintain control over their territory. The great Chepstow Castle was built on a strategic site, bounded to the north and east by the River Wye. Close by, in a quiet meadow, lie the remains of lovely Tintern Abbey, a monastery that dates from the 13th century. The abbey's roofless walls are as inspiring a sight today as they were when Wordsworth wrote his famous poem entitled "Lines Composed a Few Miles Above Tintern Abbey."

The bustling port city of Cardiff on the south coast was once notorious for its belching smokestacks and rundown docks and warehouses. Today, however, the air is clean, the waterside areas have been reclaimed, and Cardiff is showing a brighter face to tourism. Thousands of daffodils, the national symbol of Wales, brighten the grassy expanse of the War Memorial.

▲ *Caernarfon: Birthplace of Edward II, the first English Prince of Wales, Caernarfon Castle saw the investiture of Prince Charles with the same title in 1969.*

▲ *Tal-y-llyn Lake: More sheep than people live in this sparsely settled region of northern Wales, where verdant hills ring the waters of this lovely lake near Dolgellau.*

One of its most interesting historical buildings is Cardiff Castle, built on the ruins of a Roman fort whose walls are still visible. Most of the castle was built in 1093, but its clock tower and numerous banquet halls were added in the last century. On the outskirts of the city, the Welsh Folk Museum in St. Fagans offers a glimpse of life as it was lived in Wales centuries ago. Using only traditional methods, a cooper makes wooden casks, a wood-turner produces bowls and ladles, and weavers operate a water-powered loom.

The town of Caerphilly to the north, though small in size, is known for the massive fortification built in the 13th century. Caerphilly Castle is one of Britain's largest surviving medieval fortresses, surpassed in size only by Dover and Windsor. The castle ghost, the Green Lady, is said to haunt its lonely halls. She was a French princess who fell in love with a Welsh nobleman and was sent into exile by her husband, the Norman Lord of Caerphilly.

Westward along the coast is Carmarthen, set in a land of ruined castles and romantic legends. The great wizard Merlin was supposedly born in this town; on the outskirts is Merlin's Hill, where the old magician is said to be locked away in enchanted sleep. Merlin's Oak is a tree trunk over which he once cast this spell: "When Merlin's oak shall tumble down, Then shall fall Carmarthen town." To prevent such an end, the tree was set in concrete and wrapped in iron bands.

The nearby fishing village of Laugharne was for 16 years the home of the legendary poet Dylan Thomas. The little boathouse where he lived with his wife, Caitlin, and their children is open to the public; an audio-visual presentation features a tape of the poet reading his own works. Anyone expecting a solemn study lined with leatherbound volumes will be amused by the shack next door, where Thomas worked. A rickety wooden chair, humble kitchen table, pictures pinned to the wall and paper crumpled on the floor are reminders of Thomas dissolute behavior. Though the poet died during a visit to the United States in 1953, his body was returned here to be interred in Laugharne's little churchyard.

The sea cliffs that rise majestically along the southwest tip of Wales are so spectacular that in 1952 the coastline was named a national park. Here sheltered coves are interspersed with ragged, sea-lashed headlands. The offshore islands provide breeding grounds for grey seals and thousands of seabirds.

▲ St. David's: The arcaded parapets of the ruined
Bishop's Palace face St. David's Cathedral, dedi-
cated to the patron saint of Wales. The church's
simple exterior belies the lavish decoration inside.

The town of St. David's, near the westernmost point of Wales, has a cathedral; therefore it is called a city, even though its population of less than 2,000 hardly seems to warrant it. And while most cathedrals are situated to dominate the surrounding countryside, 12th-century St. David's church was set in a grassy hollow just below the town. Inside this holy spot, the bones of St. David, patron saint of Wales, rest in a casket behind the altar.

Farther up the western coast the land is gentler, with fine beaches and a scattering of quiet resort towns. This area is the most sparsely populated in England and Wales; there are no industrial towns, and the thickly wooded valleys and winding ravines in the interior show few signs of human habitation.

Here in the heart of central Wales is the lovely resort and university town of Aberystwyth. A lively seafront promenade faces the sandy beaches of Cardigan Bay, and the grounds of a ruined castle above it are laid out in public gardens. The University College of Wales at Aberystwyth lists such renowned alumni as Prince Charles. The National Library of Wales is here, too; it houses more than two million books and three million documents relating to Welsh language.

Aberystwyth is a mecca for railway buffs, for British Rail's last steam locomotives operate a tiny train line that runs 12 miles from the town to Devil's Bridge. The narrow-gauge track climbs 600 feet up beautiful Rheidol Valley to a series of spectacular waterfalls on the Mynach River.

▲ *Swallow Falls: In the heart of Snowdonia, a magical waterfall laces the densely wooded hills of Gwydyr Forest.*

To the north of Aberystwyth begins the rugged mountain scenery that is typical of northern Wales. Much of the county of Gwynedd lies in Snowdonia National Park, a land of wild peaks with sheer precipices towering over mirrorlike lakes. Fourteen mountains more than 3,000 feet high have drawn generations of climbers; in fact, the first men to scale Mount Everest trained here in Snowdonia.

The rousing song "Men of Harlech" commemorates the bravery of soldiers who defended nearby Harlech Castle during a siege in the 15th-century Wars of the Roses. The castle was one of a great string of fortresses built by Edward I around 1283. Freedom fighter Owen Glendower held it briefly in 1404 during the country's last great rebellion.

Between 1401 and 1404, Glendower also made two efforts to capture sturdy Caernarfon Castle near the northern coast, but was unsuccessful both times. Caernarfon, another castle founded by Edward I, was the birthplace of Edward's son, who became the first English Prince of Wales. Because of this connection, the castle has twice been used as a ceremonial site. In 1911 the Duke of Windsor (then Prince Edward) and in 1969 Prince Charles were invested here as Princes of Wales.

The gentle, low-lying island of Anglesey is just off the northwestern coast of Wales. Rolling green fields stretch down to the sea, and unspoiled sandy beaches line the shore. Two 19th-century bridges cross the short strait that separates Anglesey from the mainland. The graceful Menai Suspension Bridge, with a main span of 579 feet, was the world's longest bridge when it

opened in 1826. It still carries car traffic, while both trains and cars travel on the Britannia Bridge, completed in 1850.

One Anglesey town attracts scores of tourists who come to pose in front of the sign at its train station. The town's full name is reputedly the longest in the world: Llanfairpwllgwyngyllgogerychwyrndrobwllllantysiliogogogoch. Apparently, it means "the church of St. Mary by the hollow of the white aspen, near the whirlpool, and St. Tysilio's Church close to the red cave" (perhaps suggesting that it was created as a tourist attraction). The train station sells souvenirs in the form of tickets bearing the town name.

◀ *Caerphilly: Keeping tradition alive, youngsters in national costume whirl in dance beneath the forbidding walls of Caerphilly Castle, the largest fortress in Wales.*

Comfortable resort towns such as Llandudno and Colywn Bay lie along the northern coast of Wales, where sheltered coves and sandy beaches offer excellent swimming and boating. Near Conwy is one of the loveliest gardens in Britain, 120 acres laid out on a slope of the Conwy Valley. Begun in 1875, Bodnant Garden is famous for its rhododendrons, azalias, magnolias and camellias. In early summer a shower of golden laburnum blossoms forms a tunnel fringed by flowering shrubs. Later, fragrant water lilies blanket the terrace lakes, and huge beds of roses scent the air. Virtually all the trees in the exotic garden have been imported from distant lands—the monkey-puzzle from Chile, eucalyptus from Australia, the strawberry tree from the Middle East.

Southeast of here, toward the border, is the beautiful green Vale of Llangollen, a Welsh landmark since 1947. In that year the first International Musical Eistedfodd, or festival, was held here in the charming town of Llangollen. Every year since then, for a week in July, choirs, folk singers and folk dancers from all over the world have gathered here to compete under marquees erected near the banks of the River Dee. Colorful costumes brighten the grounds and the valley rings with the international language of music.

The Welsh people also celebrate their own heritage at the National Eisteddfod, held each August at a site that alternates between north and south Wales. The tradition of the Eisteddfod originated in the Middle Ages, when musicians (mostly harpists), poets and writers began gathering to compete with one another. Today the annual event has grown to embrace competitions in arts and crafts, along with the traditional choral events, pageants, speeches and poems. All the competitions are conducted in the lilting Welsh tongue, for even today the unconquerable Welsh spirit will not be dimmed by the encroachment of modern English society.

▲ Harlech: "War cries rend her hills and valleys,"ring the words to the stirring "Men of Harlech." The song refers to a desperate siege which took place at Harlech Castle during the War of the Roses.

► A glittering sea laps peacefully at this steep shore in southern Wales. Over the centuries, waves in a more violent mood have carved the coastline into jagged cliffs and arches.

IRELAND

Anchored on the far western edge of Europe, Ireland seems far removed-from the influence of the Continent's capitals, the stormy Irish Sea a barrier to the region's frequent turmoil. But the sea has long been a highway of invasion, too. First came the Celts from central Europe, overwhelming indigenous Stone Age tribes. Then the Vikings, and the Anglo-Normans, and the bloody armies of Oliver Cromwell . . . all bequeathing a legacy of conflicting cultures and competing loyalties.

The Republic of Ireland, which comprises 80 percent of the island, seems to have recently shaken off the burden of history by forging a more beneficial relationship with the Continent: membership in the European Economic Community. The EEC has provided new trade links, reducing Eire's long dependence on Britain, and infusing the once-stagnant Irish economy with billions of dollars in investment.

Pursuing a policy of rapid industrialization, the South experienced unparalleled growth in the 1970s and 1980s. Industrial output has doubled, personal incomes have soared, and Dublin has undergone its biggest building boom since the 18th century. Most telling of all, more people are returning to Ireland than are leaving it. The country now boasts the fastest-growing population in Europe, and also the youngest, with half of Ireland under the age of 25.

Still, history lives on in the very stones of Ireland, in the broken castles, the tumbled dolmen circles, the crumbled mon-

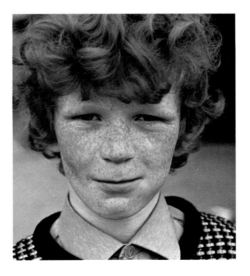

▲ Freckles and flaming red hair confirm this County Donegal lad's Irish heritage.

▲ Dunmore Head, Count Kerry: A few fallow acres, coaxed from the shallow soil, lie within a stony enclosure at the tip of the Dingle Peninsula.

asteries—the font of a people's art, and the source of much of its woe.

True Irish culture and language were brought to the island in the first century B.C. by the Gaels, a branch of the Celts who expanded throughout Europe in the centuries before the Christian era. The Celtic penchant for battle prevented unity, and resulted in 150 tribal kingdoms checkering the realm.

Roman centurions never subjugated Ireland, as they did England. A subtler, more subversive force from Rome—Christianity—conquered Ireland during the fifth century, mainly through the missionary work of St. Patrick.

Two hundred years after Patrick's death (a half-dozen towns in Ireland claim to be the saint's final resting place), Celtic Ireland was dotted with monasteries organized on a tribal basis, reflecting the ruling family's wealth. Monks developed a written Irish language, and transcribed Gaelic lore and traditions. The holy men synthesized pagan and Christian art to produce stunning illuminated manuscripts like the *Book of Kells*. Irish monks fanned out across Europe, founding monasteries in France, Switzerland and Germany, keeping the learning of Rome and ancient Greece alive during the Dark Ages. This was Ireland's Golden Age.

Then, in A.D. 795, Vikings swooped down on St. Patrick's isle and began two centuries of raids, plundering the rich monasteries of their treasures. The Norsemen eventually aligned themselves with various warring Irish chieftains, expanding trade and founding Ireland's first towns—Dublin, Wicklow, Wexford, Cork, Limerick, and many others—where they lived apart from the generally rural Gaels.

In the last half of the first millennium, ambitious chieftains consolidated their kingdoms into the realms that live on today as Ireland's four main provinces: Leinster in the east, Munster in the south, Connaught in the west, and Ulster (Northern Ireland) in the north.

A warrior named Brian Boru, King of Munster, claimed the title of High King in 1002, the first attempt to rule all Ireland. But the deeply entrenched clan system ensured that political unity remain elusive. Brian Boru did manage to end the Norse era in 1014, when he defeated a Scandinavian army at Clontarf, but the High King paid for the victory with his own life. (The battle site is just east of Dublin.)

England's fateful intrusion on Ireland's politics began by invitation in 1169, when chieftain Dermot MacMurrough petition-

ed England's French-speaking monarch, Henry II, to intercede on his behalf with Tiernan O'Rourke, an unscrupulous rival who had stolen both his kingdom and his wife. Henry permitted MacMurrough to enlist the aid of Norman nobles in Wales in exchange for control of MacMurrough's kingdom. The desperate Irish king also had to agree to give his daughter in marriage to the most powerful Norman leader of all, Richard FitzGilbert de Clare, known as Strongbow.

The Norse of the towns and the Irish of the countryside resisted the invaders at Wexford, south of Dublin, and again at Baiginbun in a series of bloody, pitched campaigns. Fewer in number but better-armed, the Anglo-Normans eventually prevailed and by 1250, controlled three-quarters of the island.

Eventually, the Anglo-Normans became more Irish than the Irish. By 1400, English law was observed and enforced only in an area around Dublin known as the Pale. Elsewhere, Irish custom prevailed (hence the term, "beyond the pale"). Still, the plantations of Elizabeth I and her successor, James I, and Cromwell's bloody campaign of conquest in the mid-1600s entrenched English power. By 1700 Protestants—20 percent of the population—owned 86 percent of Ireland.

The Anglo-Irish ruling class prospered during the following century. A violent rebellion in the late 1790s, led by the Protestant idealist Theobald Wolfe Tone—the father of Irish nationalism—failed to throw off the English yoke. Political activism was postponed by the calamitous potato famine in 1845-51, which claimed an estimated million lives and forced another million to emigrate under horrible conditions to Europe and the promised land of North America.

The disaster, along with Parliamentary maneuvers and terrorism, galvanized nationalism, which eventually brought home rule in 1914. Unrest continued despite the First World War, culminating in a bloody uprising in Easter 1916. Some 1,000 rebels seized the center of Dublin, proclaiming an Irish Republic. They were defeated only after a week of bitter fighting in which much of the center city was destroyed by fire. The execution of the leaders of the uprising further increased anti-British sentiment, and led to war in 1919. An uneasy truce ratified in 1922 partitioned the island into 26 predominantly Catholic counties—now the independent Republic of Ireland, or Eire—and six predominantly Protestant counties of Northern Ireland. It was a treaty that truly satisfied no one and the division was the start of a protracted, agonizing struggle that continues to this day.

▲ *Monasterboice: One of the best-preserved Celtic high crosses in Ireland, the tenth-century Cross of Muireadach is covered with intricately carved scenes from the Scriptures.*

▲ *Aran Island: Bundled against the cold Atlantic winds, these hardy islanders eke out a meager living on this stormy isle off the coast of Donegal.*

A Georgian Jewel

The city of Dublin owes much of its gracious appearance to the strict standards set by the Wide Streets Commission during the 1700s, Dublin's most prosperous period. The capital city's resulting broad thoroughfares lined with elegant buildings, as well as its numerous parks, churches and monuments, have withstood the forces of modernization and standardization ever since.

"Its hospitality does not exist elsewhere in Europe," wrote James Joyce of his hometown. More than a thousand pubs attest to the sociable nature of the citizens, but visitors don't have to retreat to these sudsy sanctuaries in order to savor the traditional friendliness of Dubliners.

On sunny days, cheerful sidewalk "Molly Malones," red hair blazing, hawk daffodils to passersby. The marketplace in a part of town called the Liberties (thus designated because it once lay beyond the

jurisdiction of the Lord Mayor) is so boisterous that the commerce spills out of long, shedlike buildings and into the street. Good cheer also abounds in the inexpensive restaurants of Dublin's "Left Bank," centered on Crown Alley.

Threading the heart of the city like a green strand, dividing north from south, weaves the River Liffey—Anna Liffey, Anna Livia Plurabelle, inspiration for these and other mellifluous terms of endearment. Today the Liffey is a convenient aid to direction-finding, since Dublin has no real center. Centuries ago the river was a route of invasion for the Vikings, who sailed upriver and built a stronghold here in the ninth century. Except for a brief 11th-century interlude of Celtic ascendancy, the Norsemen ruled here until Henry II conquered the city in 1170. Dublin, capital of Ireland, has belonged to invaders for most of its history.

Although the largest city in the land, Dublin remains, above all, a walker's city. The Tourist Trail outlines a zizag route past the major sites. Like the sea, Ireland's turbulent past is never far from hand. Sure enough, one of the first stops is at the General Post Office, a massive granite structure built in 1818 on O'Donnell Street, the main thoroughfare. Gutted by fire during the 1916 Easter Rising that touched off Ireland's successful drive for independence, it has been completely restored.

Just a block away from bustling O'Donnell stands an incarnation of a Dublin landmark, the Abbey Theatre. The original theater served as a music hall, bank and morgue before its walls echoed with such theatrical masterpieces as J.M. Synge's *Riders to the Sea* and Sean O'Casey's *Juno and the Paycock*. But by the early 1950s the Abbey had become so rundown that local wags nicknamed it the Shabby. When it burned to the ground in 1951, theatergoers actually rejoiced, certain that the government would fund a new facility. And so they did—only it took them 15 years to get around to it.

▲ *County Kerry: Pastures in forty shades of green extending down to the sea earn Ireland its nickname, the "Emerald Isle."*

73

Across the River Liffey, the trail leads to the sweeping, 300-foot-long facade of Trinity College, founded in 1592 by Queen Elizabeth I on the site of an ancient monastery disbanded by her father, Henry VIII. The Queen's goals for the institution were stated forthrightly: "the banishment of barbarism, tumults, and disorderly living." Treasure-house of the shady 40-acre campus is the Long Room, dating from 1732. This 209-foot-long repository contains the college's oldest volumes, including the lovingly tended *Book of Kells*, the crowning achievement of Celtic art.

Not far away, the exquisite 18th-century Merrion Square combines gracious brick-fronted Georgian townhouses with an impressive literary heritage. Oscar Wilde's parents lived at No. 1, the political hero Daniel O'Connell resided at No. 58, William Butler Yeats at No. 82. Today, the leafy 11-acre rectangle, far too expensive for poets, is home to engineers, lawyers and government agencies.

Off the west side of the square, on Leinster Lawn, stands the National Gallery. More than 2,000 works are on view, including Irish landscapes, a collection of Dutch masters, and 17th-century works of the French, Spanish and Italian schools. George Bernard Shaw, who used to play hooky in the gallery, gratefully bequeathed one-third of his royalties to his schoolboy refuge.

Nearby, on Kildare Street, stand two other important Irish institutions, the National Museum and the National Library. The buildings, both of which date from 1890 and feature a massive colonnaded entrance rotunda, flank Leinster House, seat of the Republic's parliament.

The museum is the attic of the Republic, chronicling Ireland's history since 6000 B.C. with a remarkable collection of antiquities, from a Bronze Age axehead to artifacts from the fight for independence. Some of the most impressive displays include religious items from Ireland's golden age of monasticism between the fifth and the ninth centuries: the sixth-century Tara Brooch; the heavy silver Ardagh Chalice; and the delicate Derryna flan Chalice, a ninth-century masterpiece in silver and gold, unearthed in 1980 at a monastery of the same name. There's also medieval lace from Limerick and Carrickmacross, crystal, coins and antique silver, and 12th-century treasures like the Cross of Cong, and the Shrine of St. Patrick's Bell.

Every major Irish literary figure has studied at the National Library at one time or another; a collection of first editions commemorates Yeats, Joyce, Shaw, Swift and Wilde. In his novel *Ulysses*, Joyce fictionalized the nearby Bailey Tavern as Burtons, noted for confabulators who "would sacrifice their mother for a witty phrase." The Bailey displays the door to No. 7 Eccles Street, home of Joyce's fictional hero, Leopold Bloom.

It is difficult to turn a corner without being reminded of Joyce. (Indeed, the Tourist Board publishes a literary map of Dublin that enables the writer's devoted followers to trace the meanderings of Mr.

▲ *Dublin: Brightly colored doors framed by elegant Georgian entrances belong to the aristocratic dwellings on Merrion Square, long a fashionable address in the Irish capital.*

▲ *Dublin: By barrow or by horse, the fresh produce from the surrounding countryside makes its way to one of the city's many open-air markets.*

▲ *Dublin: After a hard day's work, Dubliners love*
▲ *nothing better than to belly up to the bar for a pint of stout at one of the city's thousand-odd establishments.*

► *Almost as green as Ireland itself, the River Liffey meanders through the heart of the capital. The graceful cast-iron span in the foreground is Halfpenny Bridge, a name that recalls the days when walkers paid a toll to cross the river.*

Bloom.) In St. Stephen's Green, just south-west of Merrion Square, a bespectacled statue of the nearsighted author gazes myopically over the picnickers and strollers in this lovely urban sanctuary, which has been preserved since 1690.

Legend has it that St. Patrick converted many pagan Irish on the site of St. Patrick's Cathedral. A stone marks the spot where he reputedly struck the ground with his staff, causing pure water to gush forth for the baptizing. Most of the cathedral dates from 1190, although a 14th-century square tower and a stately 18th-century spire were added later. Author Jonathan Swift was dean of the cathedral from 1713 to his death in 1745. The author of the scathing satire *Gulliver's Travels* was tormented in his last years by a mysterious ailment that

▲ *Malahide Castle: This Norman fortress north of Dublin was in the Talbot family for 791 years. In 1976 the estate was sold to the city of Dublin; the Talbot's extensive portrait collection now hangs in the National Portrait Gallery.*

Bastions and Blarney

The county of Wexford, south of Wicklow's hills, is the heart of Ireland's "sunny southeast." Fifty pubs line the narrow lanes of the town of Wexford, founded by the Vikings as a trading post. Every October music lovers flock to the opera festival held in Wexford's gracious Georgian Theatre Royal. Earlier in the year, sun lovers bathe along six miles of beach at Rosslare.

Waterford, another Viking town, is renowned for its crystal, which gets its weight and icy sparkle from a mixture that includes 33 percent lead. The original factory opened in 1783 and closed in 1851, a sad victim of English export duties. It reopened in 1947, and now can't keep up with the orders, even with 3,000 employees. Waterford is also noted for fascinating medieval neighborhoods like Ballybricken Green, with its narrow sidestreets and passageways lined with quaint houses; for the most extensive Viking town walls in Ireland; and for Reginald's Tower, which has guarded the broad River Suir for more than a thousand years.

Ireland's best-preserved medieval town is Kilkenny, north of Waterford on the Nore River. At one end of town is the 13th-century Kilkenny Castle, surrounded by luxuriant gardens. Anchoring the other end of the Royal Mile is St. Canice's Cathedral, built in the 1200s on the site of an earlier monastery.

Irish legend traces the use of the shamrock as a symbol for the Trinity to an Easter message delivered by St. Patrick at the Rock of Cashel, southwest of Kilkenny. The rock itself, a limestone outcrop rising above the surrounding plain, is capped with the ruins of ecclesiastical structures built between the 12th and 15th centuries.

Another Irish symbol occupies a hard-to-reach niche at ruined Blarney Castle, near Cork. The pleasant prevarications of Cormac MacCarthy, Lord of Blarney, led to a deprecating comment by Queen Elizabeth I: "This is all Blarney; what he says, he never means." To inherit the lord's eloquence, a visitor must bend backward and buss the bottom-most block while hanging some 80 feet in the air.

caused giddiness and deafness. When an 1835 flood disturbed Swift's coffin in the tomb in the south aisle, Dr. William Wilde (the father of Oscar Wilde) examined the skull and diagnosed the author's problem as Ménière's Syndrome, a rare disorder of the inner ear.

Continue along the Tourist Trail north to Dublin Castle, built in the 13th century on the site of an older Danish fortification and reconstructed during the 1700s. This former symbol of British power (the English Viceroys) had their apartments here) still preserves more than 100 richly ornamented rooms. One chamber is rife with poignant associations. In it, James Connolly, a wounded leader of the 1916 uprising, awaited execution for his part in the insurrection.

◄ Dublin: The 12th-century St. Patrick's Cathedral was built on the spot where St. Patrick baptized many converts in A.D. 450. Cromwell's troops used the 300-foot church, longest in Ireland, as a stable.

▲ Glendalough Valley: Sky and summit are reflected in the tranquil waters of the Upper lake. The region's isolation inspired St. Kevin to establish a hermitage here in the sixth century.

The glories of Killarney have inspired poets and writers since the 18th century, when travelers first "discovered" the enchanting mountains, lakes and valleys of the region. The centerpiece is a lush vale cupping Killarney's three main lakes. Looming above this gentle landscape are misty mountains, including Carrantuohill, Ireland's highest summit (3,414 feet).

The famed 110-mile scenic drive called the Ring of Kerry circles Iveragh Peninsula. Starting at Killarney's purple glens, visitors drive northwest to Killorglin and then southwest to Glenbeigh, where the semicircle of seaside peaks from Seefin to Drung Hill provide one of Ireland's finest mountain walks. Glenbeigh to Cahirciveen embraces some of the most memorable scenery on the drive, with the Drung Hill on one hand and spectacular views of Dingle Bay on the other. Crossing the tip of the peninsula, the road rises sharply to meet inland mountains before descending to the sea at Derrynane Bay.

Nearby Staigue Fort, dating from about 1000 B.C., is one of Ireland's best-preserved Iron Age structures, a mortarless circular stone fort. Farther west, the road winds through wild gorges to Parknasilla. The Gulf Stream warms this coast with temperatures that rarely fall below 50°F, making it a gardeners' paradise more akin to the Mediterranean than the rest of Ireland. The road leaves the sea at the charming village Kenmare, and heads through Moll's Gap back to Killarney.

◄ Youghal: Cannons rust on the ramparts of ruined Tynte's Castle, built by the English in the 15th century in this County Cork town.

▲ *Glendalough: Among the ruins of the ecclesiatical
community that flourished in this green valley
from the sixth to the 16th centuries is a perfectly
preserved circular stone tower—a refuge from
Viking attacks.*

◄ *County Kerry: Sweaters on the hoof head for home. The dyed stripes on the back of these Merinos identify the sheep for their owners—a kind of branding, Ireland style.*

▲ *Kylemore Castle, County Galway: This magnificent turreted castle, built by Mitchell Henry in the 1860s, is now a convent of Benedictine nuns. Visitors can tour the grounds.*

The Dingle Peninsula inspires the same breathless admiration as the Killarney Lakes. Visitors return for the changeless beauty of its storm-lashed western headlands; its welcoming seaside towns; its hills and dales; its bohareens, the tiny roads winding between fields brightened with fuchsia and foxglove.

A spectacular drive north from Dingle through Connor Pass recalls the reaction of John Millington Synge, who wondered why anyone was left in Dublin, London and Paris. Wouldn't it be better to live in Dingle, speculated the playwright, "with this magnificent sea and sky, and to breathe this wonderful air, which is like wine in one's teeth."

When Oliver Cromwell came to Ireland to quell an uprising in the mid-1600s, he vowed to drive rebellious Catholics "to

▲ *The horse and wagon are still important means of conveyance in the Irish countryside.*

hell or Connaught." In the mind of this fearsome Englishman, the equivalent of Purgatory was one of the four kingdoms of pre-Norman Ireland, west of the River Shannon.

There, the exiles who wouldn't bend their knee to a foreign lord withstood a punishing climate to eke out a living from the thin, rocky soil, throwing up a tracery of stone walls that still web the isolated countryside.

The River Shannon, longest waterway in the British Isles, flows 170 miles through the heart of Ireland, rising in the north near Ulster, broadening into a series of lakes as it winds south, and emptying into a wide estuary. Invading Norsemen knew a strategic spot when they saw one, and founded the city of Shannon near the mouth of the river.

Centuries later, the first transatlantic airplane flights landed at Shannon Airport for refueling. A barman at the terminal invented Irish coffee to revive weary passengers from North America. Anticipating the day when long-range jet planes would bypass the airport, city planners "invented" the first duty-free zone, attracting dozens of international firms to the taxless manufacturing haven.

Stony County Clare is dotted with some 900 castles. Just outside Shannon, the grey hulk of Bunratty Castle, restored to its medieval splendor, whisks visitors back to the days when knighthood was in full flower. Colleens in 15th-century dress wel-

◄ *Lough Gill, County Sligo: this romantic lake with its many wooded islets inspired Yeats to write his classic poem, The Lake Isle of Inishfree.*

▲ *Aasleagh Falls, County Mayo: This cataract on the Erriff River doesn't stop salmon in their spring swim to spawning grounds farther upstream.*

come one and all with the traditional bread of friendship (Irish brown bread and salt), then seat guests around a groaning banquet table laden with traditional fare.

The often dramatic scenery of western County Clare has long been celebrated in music by the region's renowned fiddlers and step-dancers. The Cliffs of Moher rise up to 700 feet out of the sea in a five-mile palisade northwest of Liscannor, "Keeping position like broken heroes, with waves breaking upon them like time," in the words of poet Louis MacNeice.

The Burren, a strange, lunar-looking area to the northeast, is pocked with potholes and seasonal lakes which appear

and disappear. General Ludlow, who led Cromwell's forces to this area in 1651 said of the eerie 100-square mile expanse, "There is not water enough to drown a man, wood enough to hang one, or earth enough to bury him." Beneath the rock extend miles of limestone caves, including Ailwee Cave, which is open to the public.

North of Clare is County Galway, where the ancient province of Connaught begins. The market city of Gort, just across the county line, has a strong literary association with the Irish renaissance of the late 19th and early 20th centuries. William Butler Yeats lived near Gort at Ballylee Castle, one of 32 Norman towers built here by the de Burgo family.

Yeats purchased the tower, two cottages and a walled garden for £35. Yeats had discovered the castle during one of his visits to Lady Augusta Gregory at her home, Coole House, now destroyed. Fortunately, the grounds of Coole House have been maintained, with lovely forest walks and flower gardens. A prominent promoter of the Celtic revival and Yeats' patron, Lady Gregory asked house guests to sign her "autograph tree." The initials of George Bernard Shaw, John Masefield, Augustus John and other luminaries of the day can still be recognized.

Galway, that "most Irish of towns," was founded 1,100 years ago by Celts at the head of Galway Bay. Long Ireland's window on the Atlantic, the city was enriched in medieval times by a flourishing wine

trade with Spain, a connection still remembered in its Spanish Parade and Spanish Arch. Legend has it that Christopher Columbus prayed at the Church of St. Nicholas of Myra, built in 1320, before setting off for the New World.

County Galway's harshness yields to the softer beauty of Sligo. This is Yeats country, where the poet spent much of his childhood. The memory of an island in Lough Gill inspired his poem, "The Lake Isle of Innisfree." In a churchyard in Drumcliff, a gray stone slab bears the epitaph that Yeats penned for himself:

Cast a coly Eye
On Life, on Death.
Horseman, pass by.

Inhabited continuously for some 4,000 years, Sligo is also rich in prehistoric monuments. One of Europe's largest concentrations of megalithic tombs, some 65 in all, are found on a low hill at Carrowmore, three miles southwest of Sligo Town. Nearby Mount Knocknarea is capped by an unopened cairn gravesite 200 feet in diameter and 80 feet high which reputedly belongs to Queen Maeve, who ruled 2,000 years ago.

Across a narrow neck of land traversed by the River Erne lies the wild northern county of Donegal, part of Ulster province before the partition of Ireland in 1922. The "tweed villages" of Glenties, Ardara and Kilcar abound in outlets selling Donegal's famous homespun tweeds and hand-knitted sweaters. At nearby Killybegs, a factory open to visitors produces hand-tufted carpets that cover floors in the White House and the Vatican.

About 20 miles north of the "tweed villages" is a remarkable area known as The Rosses, 60,000 acres of boulder-strewn landscape watered with streams and lakes teeming with trout. (Burtonport on the coast, gateway to The Rosses, claims to land more salmon and lobster than any other port in Ireland.)

Farther north, Glenveagh National Park embraces 24,000 acres of the rugged Derryveagh Mountains. This densely wooded park, a striking contrast to the barren coast, is one of the splendors of Donegal. Streams and waterfalls splash the flanks of mountains rising sharply from the dark waters of Lough Beagh, which twists through a deep, five-mile-long gorge.

► *Ballylee Castle, County Galway: Yeats bought and restored this ancient tower, along with two cottages and a walled garden, and wrote many of his finest works here.*

▲ *County Galway: Legend has it that the famous Connemara ponies are descended from Andalusian horses carried on board ships in the Spanish Armada. Many vessels in the fleet sank along these shores, but some steeds swam to safety.*

▲ *Dunguaire Castle, County Galway: This 16th-century castle, about 40 miles north of Shannon, is the scene of nightly medieval banquets, complete with wenches, mead and traditional Irish music.*

► *Glencolumbkille, County Donegal: Villagers hereabouts lash down their roofs to weather winter storms on Ireland's wild western shore.*

ULSTER

The ancient kingdom of Ulster, a powerful citadel of Gaelic culture, was the last of Ireland's four provinces to surrender to English troops during the Anglo-Norman invasion. Ironically, when James I tried to populate Ireland with loyal subjects 500 years later by establishing vast plantations on confiscated Irish land, his only success was in Ulster. By 1640, Protestant Scots and English formed the majority of landholders. When Ireland was divided by the British Parliament in 1920, six of the nine Ulster counties became part of the United Kingdom as Northern Ireland. Today, two-thirds of the North's 1.5 million people are Protestant—and fiercely loyal to Britain.

The capital, center of industry, and chief port is Belfast, whose very name conjures up reminders of the sectarian violence that has long plagued this troubled land. Since the 1969 riots between Catholics and the Protestant majority, more than 2,000 people have been killed in bombings and assassinations. A "peace line" of steel and concrete in West Belfast demarcates the Protestant and Catholic neighborhoods; between is a bombed-out no-man's-land of deserted buildings and rubble.

And yet, on the other side of the green bowl of hills that enclose the city are the sparkling waters of Lough Neagh, largest lake in the British Isles, seemingly far removed from strife. Farther west, fishermen land salmon, trout and pike from peaceful Lough Erne and Upper Lough Erne, two of the loveliest lakes in the world, and a mecca for boaters and hikers. In the rolling countryside, the farms are small and green, with mossy stone walls enclosing herds of sleek cattle. In Londonderry County rise the wild Sperrin Mountains, a high and desolate moor covered with rocks and sparse heather.

The most spectacular scenery in Northern Ireland lies along the Antrim Coast Road, which was begun as a make-work project in 1833. The cliff-hugging highway extends between Larne, northeast of Belfast, and Portstewart, east of Londonderry. En route, the thoroughfare cuts across the Glens of Antrim, nine lush valleys running down to the sea between Larne and Ballycastle. These verdant vales intersect the black basalt cliffs and white outcroppings of the coast.

► *The forces of nature, and not of titans, built the basaltic columns of the Giant's Causeway.*

The road arches west near the Giant's Causeway, a cluster of cathedral-like columns crowning a headland. This scenic wonder was formed some 60 million years ago, when lava flowing from volcanic upheavals cooled and split into thousands of hexagonal basalt shafts.

Legend provides a more imaginative explanation. An Irish giant named Finn MacCool wanted to battle his Scottish counterpart, Finn Gall, so he built a causeway all the way to Scotland (at its closest point, Scotland lies only 13 miles from Eire across the North Channel). The work tired out MacCool so he went home to rest. His Scottish rival crossed over to Ireland on the causeway and went to MacCool's house, where the bushed bridge builder was fast asleep. Finn Gall asked Mrs. MacCool, who was sweeping the floor, if that was her husband beneath the blankets.

"Him?" replied the giant's spouse. "Sure, that's only me wee baby."

Gall decided that if the baby was that big, imagine the size of the father. He beat a hasty retreat to Scotland, ripping up the causeway behind him as he went. What visitors see today are the remains of MacCool's basalt bridge, extending only about 200 yards offshore.

Londonderry, Northern Ireland's second city, has the most complete set of city walls in Ireland. Founded in 1613 as the seat of a plantation established by the London Corporation, the small settlement was encircled by massive stone battlements within six years. They have withstood three major sieges over the centuries, and now provide a pleasant, mile-long promenade with close-up views of the city's many bastions, gates and cannon emplacements. The Anglican St. Columb's Cathedral was built in the unadorned style known as "Planter's Gothic in 1633." The more flamboyant Catholic Cathedral of St. Eugene's was erected two centuries later. Artifacts salvaged from a Spanish Armada ship, wrecked nearby in 1588, are displayed in Magee University College.

Ulster has been populated by waves of Celts, English and Scottish, but it was an unwilling immigrant who had the greatest impact on Ireland. Around A.D. 403, a raiding party of Ulster pirates sailed across the Irish Sea and captured, among other things, a teen-age British boy. They brought him back to Ulster, and set him to herding sheep in what is now Antrim.

The slave called himself by the Roman name Patricius, later shortened to Patrick. He tended his flocks for six years, then escaped as a stowaway on a ship bound for France. There, and later in Britain, he studied to become a priest. Then, in a vision, he heard Irish voices calling him to return to Eire. Patrick had himself assigned as a missionary in A.D. 432, landing in County Down.

The county's soft green Mountains of Mourne are dotted with reminders of the saint, including several "authentic" burial spots. A granite slab outside St. Patrick's Cathedral in the town of Downpatrick marks one site.

Patrick built his own cathedral in A.D. 444 atop one of the seven hills of Armagh, one of Ireland's most ancient cities. Today, Armagh serves all of Ireland as ecclesiastical seat for both the Roman Catholic Church and the Church of Ireland. It has two archbishop's palaces and two magnificent St. Patrick's Cathedrals. The Protestant structure stands on the hilltop site of the saint's cathedral. For 1,500 years, despite war and revolution, services have been held in a succession of churches on this hallowed ground.

▲ *Belfast: An uneasy peace, often interrupted by sectarian violence, hangs over the capital of Northern Ireland.*

GREAT BRITAIN • IRELAND: A Visitor's Guide

Planning a trip to Great Britain and Ireland should be a source of immense pleasure. But the hard part is deciding which sights to see—and which to reluctantly leave out. These islands are so bountiful in history, culture and natural beauty that it would take a lifetime to discover it all. Some travelers on return visits try to narrow it down, organizing their trip around a theme: perhaps the great houses of England, or Britain's historic waterways, Scotland's finest golf courses or historic pubs of Ireland. Another way, of course, is to leave it all to chance. For almost anywhere one travels in these charming islands, there are fascinating sights to see, and warm, friendly people to share them with.

NORTHERN ENGLAND ■
SOUTHERN ENGLAND ■
SCOTLAND ■
WALES ■

TOURING ENGLAND, SCOTLAND & WALES

How to get there

A number of airlines provide direct flights from most major cities in the United States and Canada to London's Heathrow and Gatwick airports. Two other British destinations from overseas are Manchester and Glasgow; these have less frequent service. Because of air-fare price wars, flights to Britain are frequently the cheapest of any European destination. And charter flights and package tours often offer substantial savings over regularly scheduled flights. For those in a hurry, to whom money is no object, the Concorde (British Airways and Air France) provides luxury service between London and New York, Washington and Miami—at half the time.

Anyone with both time and money to spare could travel by boat. Only two cruise ships make regular crossings between North America and Great Britain: Cunard's luxurious *Queen Elizabeth II* , which sails from New York to Southampton, England; and the Polish Ocean Lines' more modest *Stefan Batory* , which stops in London on its way from Montreal to Gdynia, Poland.

U.S. and Canadian citizens visiting Great Britain require only a valid passport. No entry visa or health certificate is needed.

When to go

Britain's regular tourist season runs from mid-April to mid-October. During most of that time, the temperatures are neither too hot nor too cold. Heat waves are virtually unheard-of: In summer in London the thermometer seldom climbs above 75°F, and evenings can be cool. Visitors should be prepared for rain throughout the year.

Since most of the British take their vacations in July and August, hotels in the popular resorts tend to be heavily booked during those months. September and October can be the best times to visit the northern moors and Scottish highlands; they're at their most colorful in fall. But in general, the farther north and west you go in Britain, the more it rains. Even in summer, a day rarely goes by in Edinburgh without some rainfall.

Off-season travel can be economical in Britain. While some of the lesser tourist attractions are closed, the major ones remain open and are considerably less crowded. And London's lively cultural scene is especially active in winter. The climate remains temperate: London winters see few days with the temperature below freezing. But instead of snow, it rains, and the dampness and lack of central heating in British homes can make the weather seem colder to North Americans.

Average temperatures in °F (low-high)

CITY	JAN	APR	JULY	OCT
London	36-45	40-56	56-72	45-58
Brighton	43-49	43-56	58-65	47-52
Liverpool	36-45	41-52	56-67	47-56
Cardiff	36-45	41-56	54-68	47-58
Edinburgh	34-43	40-52	52-65	45-54
Inverness	34-43	38-50	52-63	43-54

Costs

Though Britain recently ranked among the costliest of European countries for travelers, expenses are falling, and the healthy exchange rate on the U.S. dollar can make it a travel bargain for Americans.

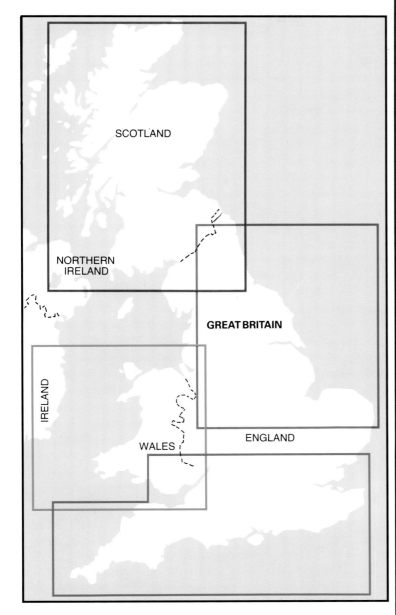

food that's far from exceptional. But bargains are available. The hearty breakfasts served at bed-and-breakfasts can keep a tourist going for much of the day, while pub lunches and fish-and-chip shops provide inexpensive sustenance.

Currency

The pound sterling is made up of 100 pence (written "p"). Bank notes are available in denominations of £50, £20, £10 and £5. Coins are in values of £1, 50p, 20p, 10p, 5p, 2p and 1p. Scotland issues its own bank notes (including a pound note) but they are completely interchangeable with English money. Wales uses only English currency.

The best place to change foreign currency is at a bank. You're guaranteed the current exchange rates, and the commission charged is small.

Medical services

Britain's National Health Service will provide free medical treatment to a tourist only at a hospital, and only in the case of an emergency. If you have to be admitted to hospital, or treated for an existing illness or condition, you must pay the bill. You'll also be required to pay a doctor who makes a "house call" to your hotel. (The hotel should have a list of doctors willing to provide this service.) It makes sense to take out adequate medical insurance, or extend your existing coverage, beforehand.

Many people find that planned package tours are the easiest way to keep costs down. Since packagers negotiate prices on a high-volume level, they can secure low rates not available to individuals. And not all package tours involve being herded from one overcrowded tourist sight to the next. They run the gamut from a trip in which everything is arranged for you—transportation, hotels, meals, sightseeing, even tips—to a simple plan providing the transatlantic flight and car rental. Those opting for an escorted package can expect to pay anywhere from $300 to $450 for a six-day bus tour around England, depending on the quality of hotels.

Tourists traveling on their own will find a wide range of accommodations to choose from. A double room in a deluxe international hotel in London will cost around $150 a night. At the opposite end of the scale is the bed-and-breakfast, for about $10 or $12 per person per night. A moderately priced hotel outside London may charge about $50 a night for a double room with bath and breakfast.

Restaurant dining can be pricey: It's easy to spend $35 per day per person on

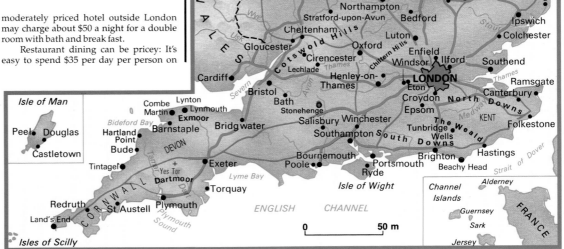

travel on seven of the eight "Great Little Trains," most of them pulled by steam locomotives. They can be bought in Wales.

Though it may not be the fastest way to get around Britain, bus travel is certainly the cheapest. On average, a bus ticket costs about half the price of a train ticket between the same two points. Long-distance buses (called "coaches" here) will take you almost anywhere you want to go. The government-sponsored National Express offers a Rapide service with luxury air-conditioned coaches, and hostesses serving food and drinks. Their BritExpress Card gives overseas visitors a one-third discount off coach fares over a 30-day period.

You can rent a car in Britain if you have a valid driver's license and proof of liability insurance. Most of the rental firms have standard contracts. It is wise to arrange the rental before leaving North America, through either your travel agent, an international rental agency, or a fly/drive package with your airline or charter company. In general, if you shop around, you'll pay less this way than if you rent after your arrival in Britain.

But however you set it up, renting a car is not a cheap way to travel in Britain. It costs more than it does in North America, and if you want a large car the price goes up accordingly. Since few European cars have automatic transmission, you'll pay extra for that if you need it. And gas prices are considerably higher.

British Airways and a number of smaller airlines provide an extensive network of air routes throughout Great Britain. Shuttle services operate between the most popular destinations, London and Manchester, Glasgow and Edinburgh. British Airways offers a Discover Britain Airpass to overseas visitors, allowing up to eight separate journeys in England and Scotland over a one-month period, with certain restrictions. The pass must be purchased in North America.

Much of Great Britain, with its rolling hills and traffic-sparse secondary roads, is suitable for bicycle touring. Changeable weather is the chief liability. But the leisurely pace of a bike trip is ideal for exploring the picturesque countryside.

Bikes can be rented in most cities and towns, and excellent detailed maps are available to help you locate the most scenic—or perhaps the flattest—routes. The Cyclists' Touring Club can also provide invaluable information on routes and organized tours throughout Britain. (Write them at: Cotterell House, 69 Meadrow, Godalming, Surrey GU7 3HS, England.) Many trains carry bicycles for free.

Shopping

Some of the best things to buy in Britain are fine china, such as Wedgwood, Royal Doulton or Staffordshire; and fine woolens: Harris tweeds, Scottish tartans, Fair Isle sweaters. While there is no local sales tax, a 15-percent Value Added Tax (VAT) is tacked on to all purchases. As a tourist, if you buy items for more than £75, you're entitled to a refund of the VAT. Show the sales clerk your passport and ask him or her to fill out a refund form, which you will then present to Customs on your departure. The refund will later be forwarded to you, or credited to your charge card. You can also have the store send the goods home for you, get the North American Customs to certify the same form, and mail it to the store yourself for your refund.

For more information

United States:
British Tourist Authority
40 West 57th St., New York, N.Y. 10019

875 North Michigan Ave., Suite 3320, Chicago, IL 60611

612 South Flower St., Los Angeles, CA 90017

Plaza of the Americas, North Tower, Suite 750, Dallas, TX 75201

Canada:
British Tourist Authority,
94 Cumberland St.,
Suite 600, Toronto,
Ont. M5R 3N3

Britain:
British Tourist Authority, Thames Tower, Black's Rd., London W6 9EL

English Tourist Board,
26 Grosvenor Gardens,
London SW1W ODU

Scottish Tourist Board,
23 Ravelston Terrace, Edinburgh EH4 3EU

Wales Tourist Board, Brunel House,
2 Fitzalan Rd., Cardiff CF2 1UY

Public holidays

The following days are celebrated as public holidays in England and Wales: New Year's Day, Good Friday and Easter Monday, May Day, Spring Bank Holiday (late May), Summer Bank Holiday (late August), Christmas and Boxing Day. In addition, Wales honors its patron saint, St. David, on March 1. Scotland adds January 2, does not observe Easter Monday, and has its bank holidays at slightly different times.

Getting around

Great Britain has one of the best railway networks in the world. It reaches just about every part of the country, is safe, fast (though not necessarily on time) and comfortable. British Rail's new high-speed Inter City 125 trains (so named because they travel at speeds up to 125 miles an hour for long stretches) lead from London to all the main centers.

Reservations are advisable, especially during tourist season and on heavily traveled routes. Fares are calculated not just on the distance traveled, but on the quality of accommodations chosen. Many trains have first-class and second-class cars. First- class seats, which are generally more spacious, cost about 50 percent more than second-class. Most of the Inter City trains have a restaurant car or at least a simple buffet car.

Night trains going longer distances, such as to Scotland, northern and western England, and Wales, offer sleeping accommodations. These must be reserved as far in advance as possible.

Anyone planning to leave London by train should be aware that the city has 11 principal train stations. It's important to find out in advance which one your train is leaving from. All are connected to the Underground (subway line) and bus routes.

The best bargain is the BritRail Pass, which allows unlimited travel anywhere in England, Scotland and Wales. These are issued for periods of one, two, three or four weeks, and can be purchased for first-class or economy travel. In most cases young people and senior citizens are entitled to reduced rates. Since the pass is only available to overseas visitors, you must make arrangements before your arrival in Britain.

Anyone traveling extensively in northwestern Scotland would find the Scottish Highlands and Islands Travelpass a worthwhile investment. It covers the fares for any ferry or bus transportation necessary to link up points on the rail system, as well as travel to the Orkney and Shetland islands and the Outer Hebrides.

Special tourist tickets are available for train buffs wanting to sample the quaint narrow-gauge railways of Wales. These passes are good for seven days' unlimited

TOURING IRELAND

How to get there

A number of scheduled flights to the Irish Republic leave from major departure points in the United States. Ireland's Aer Lingus offers frequent service from New York and Boston, with flights landing first at Shannon International Airport in western Ireland and terminating at Dublin in the east.

Charter flights are frequently available, and offer good value, as do package tours. In fact, the price of a package tour can be so favorable that it's worth paying for the entire package—flight, hotels and whatever else is offered—and using only the flight portion, if being squired around with a group of your fellow countrymen isn't your idea of the best way to see Ireland. A travel agent can best advise you.

There are no direct scheduled flights between North America and Northern Ireland, and only a few charter flights in summer. Generally the best approach is to fly to Shannon or Dublin, and continue by connecting flight to Belfast.

U.S. and Canadian citizens need no visa to visit Ireland, only a valid passport.

When to go

May and June are generally the sunniest months in Ireland, although the weather is unpredictable at any time of year. The Emerald Isle comes by its fabled green thanks to frequent rainfall—often more a heavy mist than a real downpour. Hotel rates are lowest from January through March, the months when many tourist attractions are closed, and the weather can be dank and gloomy.

Average temperatures in °F (low-high)

CITY	JAN	APR	JULY	OCT
Belfast	36-43	40-54	52-65	45-56
Dublin	34-47	40-56	52-68	43-58
Killarney	41-50	45-56	54-70	49-59

Costs

As in Britain, with the favorable exchange rates the U.S. dollar is going farther in Ireland. Package tours may be the easiest way to enjoy a holiday, but people traveling on their own will find they can enjoy a comfortable trip without undue concern.

A double room at a good hotel in Dublin might cost no more than $45-55, while a bed-and-breakfast will set you back about $25 a night for two. And the breakfasts are substantial—perhaps the best food bargain in Ireland. The Irish Tourist Board has organized a Tourist Menu program in which participating restaurants offer meals at bargain prices.

In general, prices are lower in Northern Ireland than they are in Great Britain or the Republic of Ireland. (Many Irish cross the border to do their grocery shopping in Northern Ireland's supermarkets.) The strong U.S. dollar makes prices even more favorable for Americans seeking travel bargains abroad.

Since most hotels and restaurants add a 12-to 15-percent service charge to the bill, tipping is not really necessary at these establishments. Otherwise, a tip of 10 to 15 percent is appropriate, though generally there are few occasions in Ireland when it's necessary. As a rule, don't tip in pubs.

Currency

The unit of currency in the Republic of Ireland is the pound or punt, divided into 100 pence. Since the Irish pound is linked to EEC currencies, it is not interchangeable with British money. To avoid confusion with the British pound, it is written IR£. Paper notes are distributed in denominations of £100, £50, £20, £10, £5 and £1; coins in denominations of 50p, 10p, 5p, 2p, 1p and 1/2p. U.S. dollars and British money might be accepted in larger centers, but you'll get the best exchange rates if you go to a bank.

Northern Ireland's currency is the British pound sterling, also divided into 100 pence. The exchange is more favorable if you buy pounds sterling with U.S. dollars than with Irish punts . In general, Irish currency is not accepted in establishments in Northern Ireland.

Medical services

If you become ill while traveling in the Irish Republic, you'll have to pay for any treatment you receive, even in an emergency. The General Medicine Service provides free health care only to Irish citizens or tourists from Common Market countries. Make sure you're properly covered by insurance before you leave home. Northern Ireland provides tourists with the same coverage as in Great Britain.

Public holidays

The Irish Republic observes these dates as public holidays: New Year's Day, March 17 (St. Patrick's Day), Good Friday and Easter Monday, bank holidays in June, August and October, Christmas, and St. Stephen's Day on December 26. Northern Ireland celebrates New Year's, St. Patrick's Day, Good Friday and Easter, May Day, bank holidays in May and August, Orangemen's Day on July 12, and Christmas and Boxing Day on December 25 and 26.

Getting around

Ireland's rail network, though fairly extensive, does not cover the whole country. But the trains are generally comfortable, reliable and reasonably inexpensive. And if there's no train to get you where you want to go, there's almost always a bus (here called a "coach") that will—at a far cheaper price. In general, coach fare in the Irish Republic costs about two thirds what you'd pay for a train ticket to the same destination. The government-owned National Transpor tation Company (called CIE for Coras Iompair Eirann) operates a well-integrated system that includes both trains and intercity coaches.

There are two classes of travel on Irish trains: standard and super-standard. Be-

cause of the short distances involved, there are no sleeping cars, but most trains have either a restaurant or buffet car.

If you're traveling by train throughout Europe, a Eurailpass can be a real bargain. While this pass is not accepted on the trains of Great Britain or Northern Ireland, it is good for unlimited train travel in the Irish Republic. If you intend to take trains only in Ireland, however, the Rambler Pass offered by the CIE is a better investment. It permits unlimited travel on both trains and coaches in the Irish Republic, can be purchased for eight or 15-day periods, and is available in North America or at railway stations in Ireland.

Northern Ireland also offers a train pass, called the Rail Runabout, that's good for seven days unlimited travel in Northern Ireland and is available at most railway stations. You can also buy a coach pass called the Freedom of Northern Ireland ticket. Ulster Bus, the government-owned company, also offers a wide range of sightseeing tours.

A rental car may be the best way to explore all of Ireland's nooks and crannies. In general, the roads are good, and there's so little traffic that you'll have an easy time learning to drive on the left side. To rent a car, all you need is a valid driver's licence. If you're traveling between July and September, it's imperative that you book ahead. As in Britain, gas prices are much higher than in North America. If you are renting a car in the Republic and planning to enter Northern Ireland, make sure the insurance will cover you.

In so small a country, air travel is hardly practical for a tourist bent on seeing everything. For those in a hurry, however,

flights are available on most days from Dublin to Shannon, Cork, Derry and Belfast. There is also a regular air service to the remote Aran Islands.

Road traffic is light in Ireland, and the rolling hills are pleasant, if challenging, for cycling. If you're planning to cycle in July or August you'd be wise to reserve well in advance. A bike hired in the Republic may not be ridden over the border into Northern Ireland.

For more information

United States:
Irish Tourist Board,
757 Third Ave., New York, N.Y. 10017

Northern Ireland Tourist Board, 3rd Floor, 40 West 57th St., New York, N.Y. 10019

Canada:
Irish Tourist Board, 10 King St. East, Toronto, Ont. M5C 1C3

For Northern Ireland, contact the British Tourist Authority, 94 Cumberland St., Suite 600, Toronto, Ont. M5R 3N3

Britain:
Irish Tourist Board, 150 New Bond St., London W1

Northern Ireland Tourist Board, Ulster Office, 11 Berkeley St., London W1

Ireland:
Irish Tourist Board, Baggot St. Bridge, Dublin 2
Northern Ireland Tourist Board, River House, 48 High St., Belfast BT1 2DS

PICTURE CREDITS

Credits are from left to right, top to bottom
with additional information if needed.

Cover: Daily Telegraph/Masterfile
2-3   J. Sims, Daily Telegraph/Masterfile
3   John Lewis Stage/The Image Bank Canada
6   A. Howarth, Daily Telegraph/Masterfile
7   Albano Guatti/Masterfile
8-9   Tony Stone, Worldwide/Masterfile
9   Ivor Sharp/The Image Bank Canada; Kay Chernush/The Image Bank Canada
10   Jules Zalon/The Image Bank Canada; 11 Sykes/Viva
12   Hurn/Magnum; 13 Guillemot/Top
14   Cartier-Bresson/Magnum; 14-15 Jalain/Top
16   Picturepoint; J. Bottin; 16-17 Goulston/Bruce Coleman
18   Seed/Rapho; (top) Jalain/Top; C. Lénars; 19 Clifton/Colorific
20-21   Hidalgo/Top
22   Chapman/Fotogram; (top) Maeder/Colorific; J. Verroust; 23 Picturepoint
24   Le Bastard/Explorer; 24-25 Koch/Rapho
26   Beuzen-Top; Allen/Bruce Coleman; 26-27 Barrington/Colorific
28   Daily Telegraph/Masterfile; 28-29 Tweedie/Colorific
30   Battaglia/Colorific; (top) Beuzen/Top; 31 Tweedie/Colorific
32   Desjardins/Top; P. Tétrel (2); 33 Allen/Bruce Coleman
34-35   Vernier/Explorer
36   J.-S. Roux (2); 37 B. Gérard;
38-39   Daily Telegraph; 39 Picturepoint (2)
40-41   Guillemot-Top
42   Tweedie/Colorific; Spencer/Colorific; 43 Everts/Rapho
44   Allen/Bruce Coleman; 44-45 Picturepoint
46   Berry/Magnum; 46-47 G. Malherbe
48-49   J.-S. Roux
50   Picturepoint; Bartlett/Colorific; 51 Aarons; B. Gérard
52   B. Gérard (2); 53 Desjardins/Top
54   Ducange/Top; Mayaux du Tilly/Rapho; 55 Ducange/Top
56   Desjardins/Top; Guido A. Rossi; The Image Bank Canada; 56-57 Aarons
58   Gerster/Rapho; 58-59 Sykes/Viva
60-61   Ducange/Top
62   Saint-Servan/Explorer; 63 B. Gérard
64   Allen/Bruce Coleman; 64-65 Serraillier/Rapho; 65 G. Malherbe
66   Moss/Colorific
68   Clifton/Colorific; B. Gérard; 68-69 Tweedie/Colorific
70   B. Gérard; 71 P. Tétrel; (bottom) Martel/Rapho
72   P. Tétrel (2); 73 P. Tétrel
74   P. Tétrel (3); 75 P. Tétrel
76   P. Tétrel (2); 77 Monin/Top
78   P. Tétrel; 78-79 P. Tétrel
80   Belzeaux/Rapho; 81 P. Tétrel
82   Belzeaux/Rapho; 82-83 P. Tétrel (2)
84   P. Tétrel (2); 85 P. Tétrel
86-87   P. Tétrel
88   P. Tétrel; (top) A. Gaël; 89 Guido A. Rossi/The Image Bank Canada
Back cover: Daily Telegraph/Masterfile